Discovering Wine

Written by Neil Courtier

KUDOS

Kudos is an imprint of Top That! Publishing plc.
Tide Mill Way, Woodbridge, Suffolk, IP12 IAP, UK
www.kudosbooks.com

Contents

Archaeologists have discovered evidence of winemaking taking place some 12,000 years ago. The cultivation of the vine first flourished around the Black Sea, and then the Persians helped to spread the word through Assyria. Evidence of innovation taking place in Egypt and the Mediterranean comes from Egyptian wall paintings clearly depicting scenes of growing and harvesting vines.

Introduction

Trade Origins

Today the cultural importance of wine can be seen in everyday life, particularly in countries such as France and Italy where a meal isn't really complete without a glass of wine to accompany it. In the United Kingdom and the United States, consumption and interest in the subject continues to increase.

The Greeks were probably the world's first wine merchants, while the Romans fine-tuned methods of winemaking and established vineyards throughout Europe, some of which have proved, over time, to be great sites of origin. After the Dark Ages, the church became influential, and so eventually did the monarchs of England, who shaped the wine-drinking habits of the British and started a wine trade, which today is the most diverse in the world.

There is so much to discover in the world of wine. Its study can be made unnecessarily complicated but *Discovering Wine* aims to take the mystique out of the subject. This book offers lots of practical advice and pointers towards increasing your enjoyment of what is truly a great drink.

This book is not made or authorised by the winemakers that have products featured in this book, or by anyone involved with them.

MAKING WINE

Making Wine

Many of the world's best producers believe that great wine is first created in the vineyard.

Indeed, it is difficult to argue with the suggestion that using top-quality ingredients helps when transforming grapes into wine.

White wine can be made from both white and black grapes. Crushing breaks the skins, after which de-stalking takes place. Gentle pressing is favoured and skins are removed. Fermentation traditionally happens in oak barrels, although today, when minimal change is required, most white wines will ferment in stainless steel vats. Maturation in oak barrels can add another dimension and flavour profile to a wine.

MAKING WINE

Red wine must be made from black grapes. This time the juice is fermented on the skins for better colour extraction. The juice, which runs freely after fermentation, is of the highest quality. The remaining pomace, or skins, are further crushed to release any more juice, which is generally used in blending. Maturation can, of course, be controlled in oak barrels. The filtration of red wine may be minimal, if at all.

Most fruity wines made to be consumed young will have little further maturation or development in the bottle. Some of the world's great classics however, can evolve slowly, to reach a plateau of maturity and amazing levels of complexity.

Using Oak

Oak barrels are used by a winemaker to impart complementary flavours and aromas to a wine. Barrels are toasted at various levels from light to medium to heavy, and will be selected to suit a particular grape variety or style of wine. Additional flavours can also be gained from the complex interaction with yeast 'lies' (or 'lees'), the yeast sediment which will be in contact with the wine.

Barrels are a convenient container in which to store a wine, as the subtle exchanges with oxygen, moisture and alcohol help the wine to evolve from the youthful 'green' to more complex and mature flavours.

Many different types of oak are used in the winemaking process, with white oak being the most common. French, Hungarian, and North American oak are the best-known species used, with each one having slightly different attributes. Just as vines and grapes are distinctly individual when grown under different conditions or areas, so are oak trees.

Very few wineries have their own cooperage, preferring to rely more often on purchasing barrels that have been carefully milled, cured, and toasted. It is an expensive business and requires a huge investment to be made by the barrel supplier.

Taste Test

*Why do we taste wine and
what are the advantages of
being able to taste successfully?*

Arguably, the most important factor here is to recognise when a wine is in good condition, or when a bottle is faulty.

This becomes particularly relevant when you are faced with the sort of markups applied in some restaurants. When a sample from an approved bottle is offered to taste, you are checking the condition of the wine that you have ordered, not tasting the wine to decide whether you like it!

The Three Steps

There are three simple steps to follow when tasting wine: look, smell, and taste. Firstly, you should look at the wine when it's poured. Is it clear and bright? Is it looking in good shape? An excess of brown colour in a white wine may indicate that it has gone off. It's possible to guess the age of a red wine by observing its rim colour. Tilt the glass slightly and look at the edge of the wine. If you see a purple tint it is probably a young wine while an orange tint is an indication of maturity.

Swirling the wine around the glass will release the aromas and you should take either a large sniff or a small sniff, followed by a large sniff. Does the wine smell clean and fresh and can you identify fruit-related aromas? If not, and you detect musty, wet cardboard-like aromas, you have probably found a fault. Young wines should always be fruity and appealing on the nose. You should take time to sniff the wine and not rush into tasting.

TASTE TEST

Some wine styles, for example aromatic whites such as Sauvignon Blanc, are intense and lively on both the nose and palate. Expect to be able to identify lots of fruit and primary aromas. Wines that have matured or developed in the bottle may have a bouquet and flavours such as those associated with dried fruits (prunes, figs, etc.), along with savoury nuances. Lurking among all this complexity there should still be hints of fruit. Some wines over a decade old (for example, German Riesling) will surprise you with their amazing vitality and youthful tones.

Lots of fuss can be generated when the virtues of a vintage are discussed and in some cases this is justified. As a generalisation, if a wine is made from grapes growing in a cool or marginal climate, then vintages can matter. In warmer climates, where there is better consistency in weather patterns, the changes affecting quality are far less significant.

Tasting allows you to confirm the condition and characteristics associated with the wine. You should consider the initial taste, the actual taste, and the aftertaste. Have the confidence to reject a bottle which you feel may be tainted and make sure that you assess each bottle ordered individually.

Relax

If you follow the guidelines, concentrate and relax when tasting wine, and forget the fear factor, there is no reason why you cannot become a confident taster.

White Grapes

The taste of a wine depends principally on the grapes from which it is made. Different climates, soils, and winemaking techniques also play a part. White wine is almost always made from white grapes, although black grapes can be used if contact between the skins (where colour is obtained) and the juice is avoided.

All grape varieties have individual characteristics and ripen at different times, the type of grape exerting a heavy influence on the taste of a wine.

Categories

Broadly speaking, the styles of white wine produced can be broken down into three categories: light-bodied white wines such as German Riesling, aromatic white wines such as Gewürztraminer, and full-bodied and wooded white wines such as Chardonnay or Sémillon.

Chardonnay

The world's most popular white grape, Chardonnay expresses its varietal character in many forms: from the racy, steely, and nervy wines of Chablis, to the fuller-bodied, buttery rich wine made in the Napa Valley, California.

Chardonnay could be described as a 'winemaker's dream' because it's easy to work with and produces an amazing range of flavours – lemon, pineapple, peach, apple, honey, butter, bread, hazelnut, (oak-aged) vanilla, and biscuit. The butter and creamy texture often associated with Chardonnay is a significant sign that malolactic fermentation, which softens the 'green', underripe characteristics, has occurred. Malolactic fermentation will be encouraged in cool-climate wines that may well have excess acidity but is usually avoided in warmer climates, where acidity tends to be low.

Chardonnay reaches its greatest heights in Burgundy's Côte D'Or, where the best wines, such as Meursault or Montrachet, gain sublime richness and complexity from the all-important limestone soil.

This grape's rise to stardom has been dramatic, considering that in South Australia, no Chardonnay was planted until the early 1970s. There is a danger though, that the full-bodied, buttery, fruity Chardonnay with an oaky flavour will become so popular that it may become difficult to convince consumers that a fresh, lively, oak-free version not only shows the true characteristics of the grape variety, but is an alternative to the 'international style'.

Where in the world?

The Chardonnay grape is grown in Burgundy, Champagne and the south of France, Australia, New Zealand, California, South America and South Africa.

15   WHITE GRAPES

Sauvignon Blanc

This is an aromatic grape, which ripens early and is mostly grown in cool-climate vineyards.

Its range extends from featherweight, tangy, dry white wines like Sauvignon de Touraine, to the ripe, almost tropical-like fruitiness obtained in California, where the less common addition of oak is often adopted and labelled 'Fumé Blanc'. Sauvignon Blanc thrives on chalk or gravel soils.

In France, Sauvignon Blanc finds its greatest expression at the eastern end of the Loire Valley, at Sancerre and Pouilly Fumé (Pouilly Sur Loire), but this is matched in New Zealand, particularly in the Marlborough district.

The New Zealand style – all the rage today – offers a stunning combination of zesty fruit and richer melon undertones which burst into action as soon as the cork is drawn, or indeed the cap is loosened.

In Bordeaux, a few châteaux, such as La Mission Haut-Brion and Domaine de Chavalier, lavish attention on Sauvignon, carefully blending it with Sémillon and ageing the blend in oak. These rich, lanolin-textured wines are allowed to age for decades, but most Sauvignon Blancs are consumed as young wines.

Sauvignon Blanc can play an extremely important supporting role to Sémillon, in both dry and sweet wines. This is particularly the case in Bordeaux, as Sémillon, naturally low in acidity, gains a fresh and youthful attribute from its presence.

Where in the World?

The Sauvignon Blanc grape is grown in the Loire and St Bris (Northern Burgundy) in France, New Zealand, USA, Western and South Australia, South Africa and Chile.

WHITE GRAPES

Riesling

The Riesling grape is seen by many as the most versatile variety of white grape in the world. It is without doubt a class act with a number of strengths, not least its ability to outperform Chardonnay in the longevity stakes.

As it can be harvested at various stages of ripeness, it is able to produce an amazing range of flavours, from the dry and racy expressions of northern Germany to luscious dessert wines. Riesling can reach thrilling levels of complexity, without any trace of new oak used either during fermentation or maturation, and its sheer diversity makes it compatible with a plethora of foods.

German Rieslings are some of the most difficult wines to produce, particularly when the vines are grown on the very steep slopes of the Mosel–Saar–Ruwer. So why are they so difficult to sell?

A late ripener, often resulting in wines with low to lowish alcohol, a German Riesling makes an excellent aperitif and is a perfect lunchtime drink. Exciting Rieslings are produced all over the world, reflecting the difficult soils and microclimates in which it is grown. A more full-bodied and drier version is produced in Alsace, Austria, and Australia. Alsace, sheltered by the Vosges Mountains, has a warm and dry climate. The extra ripeness in the grapes can be fermented into alcohol. They are great food wines (an Alsace Riesling is made for the table) that can also age brilliantly.

Where in the World?

The Riesling grape is grown in Germany, Austria, Alsace in France, Australia, Northern Italy, New Zealand, California, Oregon and Washington State.

WHITE GRAPES

Sémillon

Arguably one of the most underrated varieties of grape, Sémillon, Bordeaux's most widely planted white grape, makes delicious dry and sweet wines.

With an almost honeyed texture, Sémillon is often partnered by Sauvignon Blanc to lift the acidity, although Australian winemakers also blend Sémillon with Chardonnay and sometimes Trebbiano.

Some of Australia's greatest wines stem from the grapes grown in the Hunter Valley, where many of the world's longest-lived Sémillons are made.

When combined with oak, a toasty and creamy dimension is added. An oak-aged Sémillon reveals an amazing breadth of flavour and texture, with notes of burnt toast and mineral on the nose.

Sweet Sémillons with a wonderful honeyed character are produced in Sauternes, where botrytis (known as the 'noble rot') alters the complexion of the grapes by concentrating the sugar and thus intensifying levels of sweetness. Opulent in style, flavours of apricot, peach, butterscotch, and honey are achieved, and these are balanced with underpinning acidity. Australia's golden late-harvested wines also contribute to this style.

Where in the World?

Dry Sémillons are made in Australia, Chile, Bordeaux, New Zealand, South Africa, and California; while sweet Sémillons originate in Australia, Sauternes and Barsac in France, and in California.

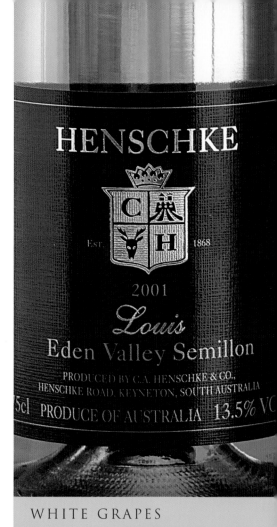

21

Chenin Blanc

An extremely versatile variety of grape, Chenin Blanc is capable of making dry and crisp white wines that are great as an aperitif, through to medium, unctuous and sweet styles.

Due to the keen and vibrant acidity often found in Chenin Blanc grape, they make brilliant food wines and can stay in good shape for many years after the vintage. The grape seems to thrive best in marginal climates, such as the Loire Valley, and on chalky soils.

Along the Loire Valley, in Vouvray, Montlouis, Anjou, Bonnezeaux, Quarts de Chaume, and Coteaux du Layon, Chenin can be hugely complex and of great character. The most amazing quality of Chenin Blanc wines is their longevity. Curiously, they become sweeter rather than drier with age. These are wines that can really benefit from bottle maturation and consequently make really good presents for christening or naming ceremonies! The best Chenin Blancs are some of the wine world's most undervalued treasures.

Less exciting wines are produced elsewhere. In South Africa for example, Chenin Blancs, known locally as Steen, often lack in complexity unless they are made from low-yielding bush vines, or the winemaking is in the capable hands of a conscientious producer. Old vine Chenin can take on another dimension when barrel fermented or aged in oak.

Where in the World?

Chenin Blanc wines are made in the Loire, Australia, New Zealand, South Africa and California. The sweet wines are found in the Loire and South Africa.

WHITE GRAPES

Other
White Grapes

GEWÜRZTRAMINER

This distinctive grape variety is known by its friends simply as Gewürtz but sometimes also as Traminer. It provides intense aromas, reminiscent of lychee, rose petals and spice. Gewürztraminer often smells sweet, but may produce an element of surprise, by tasting dry. It tends to grow best in cooler climates where there is a decent level of acidity in the soil. Alsace Gewürztraminers are the most successful, with wines from other territories tending to be bland in comparison.

Where in the World?

Gewürztraminer is found in Alsace, Germany, Northern Italy, Eastern Europe, and the USA.

MUSCADET (MELON DE BOURGOGNE)

This grape makes the seafood wine par excellence. Offering hints of apple and gooseberry, the wine becomes dry, savoury and tangy, particularly when aged in contact with the lees (sur lie) – the yeast deposit left after fermentation. Attempts to age Muscadet in oak are not guaranteed to meet with success as the grape's structure and body tend to preclude assimilation with the wood.

Where in the World?

The Muscadet grape thrives in the Loire Valley.

MUSCAT

All members of the large Muscat family share a floral, grapey, and aromatic character. Depending on when it's picked, Muscat is capable of making dry to sweet wines, from the very lightest to the biggest 'stickies', such as the Liqueur Muscats of Australia. The taste of sweet Muscats is redolent of raisins and oranges. These wines may be fortified with grape brandy during the fermentation process in order to preserve sweetness. The Muscat is often blended with other varieties of grape in order to increase complexity and flavour. It is used in the well-known Italian wine Asti Spumante.

Where in the World?

Muscat is grown throughout Europe and also in Australia.

TREBBIANO (UGNI BLANC)

The most widely planted white grape in Italy, the soil and warm climate help to create wines with highish acidity. Indeed,

WHITE GRAPES

because of its high acidity it is sometimes blended with red wines. Trebbianos tend to be medium bodied and with zesty fruit character. Trebbiano is usually fermented in stainless steel vats and may be matured in oak in order to add some complexity to the flavour.

Where in the World?

Italy and France, where the grape is used in the blend for Vin de Pays des Côtes de Gascogne. It also makes excellent distilling material for both Cognac and Armagnac.

VIOGNIER

Very aromatic, Viognier's hallmark notes are of apricot, peach, and honey. Lush and fleshy, the dry wines produced by the Viognier grape are so aromatic that they can seem sweet on the palate. Viognier is a difficult grape to grow successfully. Indeed, modern winemaking techniques are being developed to encourage a consistency in the taste. In France it tends to do best on the small hillsides outside Lyons.

Where in the World?

Viognier takes centre stage in Condrieu (Northern Rhône) and is also doing well in Southern France, Chile, Australia, and California.

MARSANNE

From the Rhône Valley, France's Marsanne makes full-bodied, fat and weighty wines, with flavours of peach and toast, and can even taste nutty when mature. Marsanne may be blended with Roussanne.

PINOT BLANC (PINOT BIANCO)

Pinot Blanc invariably makes dry, apple-scented and flavoured white wines, with a touch of honey and a whiff of spice in Alsace. Very adaptable with food, Pinot Blanc is also star material for sparkling wine.

Where in the World?

Pinot Blanc is another grape to originate in the Alsace region of France although it is now grown throughout Europe and also in North America.

Red Grapes

Red or 'black' grapes produce different levels of colour and body, the colour coming from the grape skin. Creating a light-bodied red wine depends on the amount of structure obtained from extract and tannins that the wine takes on.

These 'flavourings' provide depth and longevity. Medium-bodied wines will have a taste that may be a direct result of the grape variety or varieties used in the blend, the climatic conditions or even, in some cases, the vintage.

Body

Thick-skinned grape varieties, such as Cabernet Sauvignon, are capable of making full-bodied, dense, and long-lived wines. Winemaking also plays a part, as colour and extract can be controlled as part of the process to make wines that are well balanced and harmonious.

Light-bodied red wines include Beaujolais Primeur, medium-bodied red wines include Chinon and Barossa Valley Shiraz is among the most popular of the full-bodied red wines.

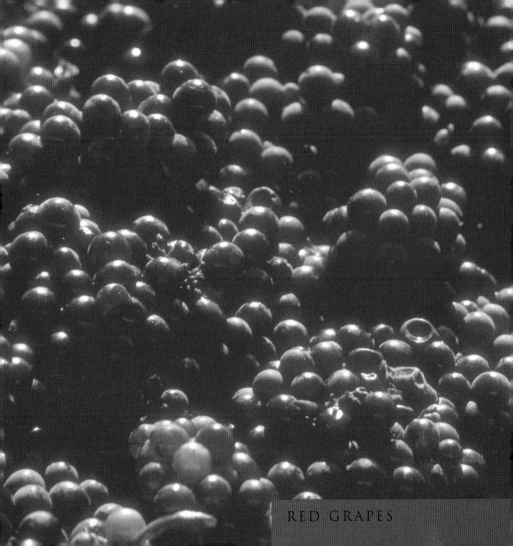

RED GRAPES

Cabernet Sauvignon

One of the world's most popular black grapes, Cabernet Sauvignon's deep colour, blackcurrant aroma and flavour is the backbone of many full-bodied red wines.

An international traveller, successful in many parts of the world, Cabernet Sauvignon is easy to grow and just loves warm, free-draining soils. It reaches great heights in Bordeaux's Haut-Médoc, as well as in the Napa Valley, Australia (Western and Coonawarra), Chile, Argentina, and South Africa.

In Bordeaux, in particular the areas of the Médoc and Graves, Cabernet Sauvignon is blended with Merlot, Cabernet Franc, Petit Verdot, and Malbec in varying proportions. Combined with new oak, for which it has a natural affinity, Cabernet Sauvignon provides the structure in a blend. In Australia, a Cabernet/Merlot/Shiraz blend has been very successful.

Cabernet Sauvignon's ability to age allows the development of cedary flavours in bottle. In young wines and those from the warmer climates cassis, mint, eucalyptus, green pepper and tarry characteristics are the norm. Of all wine grapes, Cabernet Sauvignon has one of the highest ratios between pip and pulp. As the pips are an important source of tannin, a wine based on this grape variety tends to be tough and unforgiving in youth. Blending with the softer Merlot brings accessibility as tannins soften with age and can be absorbed by particular foods.

Where in the World?

In just about every country where red wine is made.

DUCKHORN VINEYARDS

1996
NAPA VALLEY
CABERNET SAUVIGNON

Produced and bottled by Duckhorn Vineyards
1000 Lodi Lane, St. Helena, CA 94574 BWCA 4857

ALCOHOL 14.2% BY VOLUME

Merlot

A member of the Bordeaux family, Merlot, in contrast to Cabernet Sauvignon, is soft, fruity, fleshy, and less tannic.

It's the principal grape variety in the wines of St Emilion and Pomerol, and is often blended with Cabernet Franc. These Bordeaux wines are much more accessible when young, but they invariably age quickly, creating a supple, smooth, and velvety texture. Merlot is the most planted grape variety in Bordeaux.

Its characteristics tend to lean towards plum, blackberry, fruitcake, and curranty tones. In cooler climates, such as northern

Italy, grassy notes are evident. Due to its softness and moderate tannins, Merlot, which has a natural affinity with oak, is often blended with Cabernet Sauvignon.

A grape which thrives on clay and limestone-based soils, it is all the rage in California and Chile, where rich, even chocolaty Merlots are made. The dense Merlots of California can be extremely good and again can provide perfect blending material for Cabernet, as seen in the Mondavi-Rothschild icon wine, Opus One.

The relatively cool climate of New Zealand enables Merlot, in good vintages, to obtain excellent balance between fruit and acidity. In contrast, Australia's warmer vineyards are not necessarily ideal, as acidity can sometimes be found wanting, making 'cooler' Coonawarra and Western Australia more favourable locations.

Where in the World?

Bordeaux (St Emilion and Pomerol), Australia, Chile, Southern France, New Zealand, South Africa, California, and Washington State.

RED GRAPES

Pinot Noir

Pinot Noir has fewer colouring pigments (anthocyanins) than other dark-skinned varieties, so it can appear to be lighter or more aged, when compared to wines such as Malbec from Argentina which can be dark and almost inky on occasions. Of course, there are exceptions to the rule, such as the wines from the likes of Romanée Conti in Burgundy's Côte D'Or.

A difficult 'customer' described by one well-known winemaker as a 'moving target of a grape variety', on top form Pinot Noir can make the most complex and hedonistic of red wines.

Pinot Noir is a prime example of the importance of terroir, the term used to describe the growing conditions of the grape such as the soil, drainage, microclimate, and exposure to the sun.

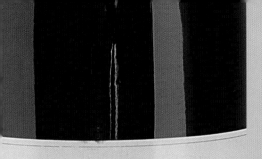

Pinot Noir is an excellent wine when the grapes have been grown in Burgundy but an altogether more challenging prospect when grown elsewhere.

Carneros and the Central Coast of California, Oregon, the Yarra Valley, and cooler spots in Australia, are consistently producing 'typical' and different expressions of Pinot Noir. New Zealand, via Martinborough, Marlborough, Central Otago and South Africa, via Walker Bay, are also now producing decent Pinot Noir.

The Pinot Noir nose is often reminiscent of raspberry, strawberry, and redcurrant when young, taking on subtle, earthy, leafy, prune-like aromas with age. It is also one of the classic Champagne varieties.

Where in the World?

Burgundy, Alsace, Champagne and Sancerre in France, Germany (Spätburgunder), Italy, New Zealand, South Africa, Switzerland, and California, Oregon and Washington State in the United States.

RED GRAPES

Syrah (Shiraz)

The Hill of Hermitage and vineyards steeply overlooking the Rhône provide the home of Syrah and one of the most famous place names associated with this great grape variety.

Hermitage, Cornas and Côte Rôtie are full-bodied red wines, while Crozes Hermitage and St Joseph are generally a touch lighter. Syrah is a hardy grape, growing well in poor soil, such as the granite-based hills and slopes of the Northern Rhône, and able to adapt to a number of climates.

In their infancy, Syrah-based wines smell of blackberry and ground pepper, sometimes mixed with aromas of smoke and toasty oak. In the Northern Rhône, Syrah is the only permitted black grape, while in the south it is used as a blending material and can be just one of several grape varieties making up the final Cuvée. Grenache is more widely grown and used in the south.

Often requiring time to develop, due to the tannic nature of young Syrah, the wines soften with age, taking on smoky, leathery characteristics. In Australia, a range of styles exist, from light to medium-bodied fruity reds, to the massively fruity, rich, powerhouse wines of the Barossa Valley. Australian Shiraz, which has captured the imagination of wine lovers throughout the world, ranges from the moderate to very expensive, such as Penfold's legendary Grange.

Where in the World?

The grape is known as Syrah in the French growing areas of the Rhône and the south of the country but as Shiraz in its other locations: Australia, Tuscany in Italy, South Africa, and California.

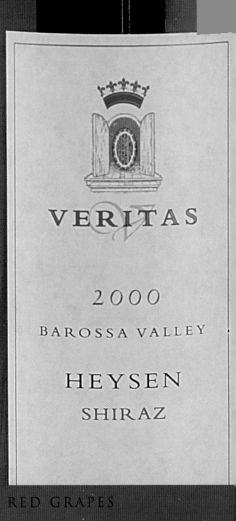

VERITAS

2000

BAROSSA VALLEY

HEYSEN

SHIRAZ

RED GRAPES

Other Red Grapes

CABERNET FRANC

Within the trio of Bordeaux varieties, alongside Cabernet Sauvignon and Merlot, Cabernet Franc is often responsible for lending an aromatic quality and positive acidity to a blend. Known for its raspberry-like aromas, it is, after Pinot Noir, the best grape of the Loire, and is used to make wines such as Chinon. Back in Bordeaux, you will find Cabernet Franc's level of importance elevated in St Emilion, no more so than in the fabulous Château Cheval Blanc. As with Cabernet Sauvignon, Cabernet Franc grows best in warmer climates but hot climates will have a negative effect on the flavour. The grape is sufficiently robust for the fermentation temperature not to be critical.

Where in the World?

Apart from Bordeaux and the Loire, Cabernet Franc is grown in Italy, the USA, Australia, and eastern Europe.

GAMAY

Gamay is the Beaujolais grape, known for its light, soft, and easy-drinking qualities. Light in tannin and full of cherry and strawberry flavour, it peaks in the Beaujolais Crus (officially classified vineyards), such as Morgon and Fleurie. In the Loire, where it is used to make red and rosé wines, Gamay accounts for about fifteen percent of all French plantings. Gamay is usually fermented through a process called maceration, where fermentation takes place below a protective layer of carbon dioxide.

Where in the World?

Gamay is grown almost exclusively in France, principally in Burgundy and the Loire Valley.

GRENACHE/ GARNACHA

The strawberry-scented and peppery tones, which often dominate a Côtes du Rhône or Châteauneuf-du-Pape, are the well-known characteristics of Grenache. At best, Grenache can reveal concentration and great power from old, low-yielding vines. The Grenache thrives in the exceptionally hot climates of Spain and the south of France. It blends well with Shiraz and is used with Tempranillo for Riojas. In Spain, where it is known as Garnacha, it is renowned for providing the colour and flavour in the fruity Rosados.

Where in the World?

As well as being planted in Spain and France the Grenache is also found in Australia and the USA.

MALBEC

The hallmark characteristics of Malbec wines are deep colour and flavours full of black fruit. The grape originates from southwest France, in the Appellation of Cahors, where the wines were once known as 'Black Wines'. Expect to find Malbec in blends too, such as in Côtes de Bourg, Bordeaux. In recent years Malbec grapes have thrived in irrigated, sandy soils in the warm climate of Argentina. Good crops combined with advances in winemaking techniques have produced some excellent, full-flavoured wines.

Where in the World?

Malbec is grown in France, Italy, Spain, South America, and the USA.

MOURVÈDRE/ MONASTRELL/ MATARO

This powerful grape variety adds blackberry-like concentration and structure to many blends. It can be truly exciting, as in Bandol, and in the tiny vineyard plantings of the southern coastal districts of California. Young Mourvèdres tend to be earthy but ageing can cause the development of a smoky aroma.

Where in the World?

Grown in the south of France, Spain and Australia, the Mourvèdre prefers a hot climate.

NEBBIOLO

The two greatest names and expressions of the magical Nebbiolo grape, Barolo and Barberesco, grow in the hills of Piedmont, Italy. Often requiring age, these are rich and savoury wines, with aromas of tar and roses! Nebbiolo is fermented in temperature-controlled stainless steel vessels. Generally, it requires a long ageing period in wood in order to soften but trends are towards shorter periods, in maceration and more bottle ageing.

Where in the World?

Apart from Piedmont, Nebbiolo is grown in California, South America, and the USA.

PINOTAGE

Pinotage, the earthy, spicy, deeply coloured grape of South Africa, has aromas of plum skin and a generous, well-structured palate. The grape is actually a hybrid of the Pinot Noir and Cinsault grapes and was created by a professor at Stellenbosch University in the 1920s.

Where in the World?

Although most associated with South Africa, attempts have been made to grow the grape in New Zealand, Chile, and Australia.

SANGIOVESE

Sangiovese, the great Italian grape, makes the concentrated red wines of Tuscany. It is the main constituent of Chiantis, the best of which are rich, plummy, cherry-scented wines, highish in acidity, and with tannins which soften towards cedary elegance with age. The lighter wines, such as the Sangiovese de Romagna, are ideal for everyday drinking. They are best drunk while young and fresh.

Where in the World?

Apart from Italy, the Sangiovese has also impressed in California, Australia and Argentina.

TEMPRANILLO

Spain's best red grape, Tempranillo is the backbone of Rioja and the wines of Ribera del Duero. Wines range in flavour from strawberry and vanilla lightness to full-bodied cherry-dominated depth. Tempranillo is also used in the production of port.

Where in the World?

The Tempranillo variety is also grown in Portugal, where it is called Tinta Roriz, and Argentina.

ZINFANDEL

Rarely seen outside of California, Zinfandel can vary enormously in style, from the bland, slightly pink 'White Zins', to old vine, oak-aged, richly fruity, elegant wines, which finish with a note of tangy acidity. Part of the explanation for the variety of Zinfandel wines lies in the fact that the very latest technology is used in production. This technology ensures that the grape rises to the challenge of adaptability.

Where in the World?

Predominantly California.

Rosé Wines

Rosé wines are made from black grapes, which are crushed and fermented with the skins until there is a little colour extraction.

The wine is drawn off the skins and completes its fermentation at a low temperature. An alternative technique is the Saignée method which is used on de-stalked grapes. These are not crushed but vatted for 12–24 hours, after which the juice is run off (bled) and fermented without skin contact.

Styles

There are some exciting styles of rosé on the market, including traditional wines such as Tavel and Sancerre Rosé, which contrast with the vibrant and fruity examples from the southern hemisphere, such as the Grenache/Shiraz blends from Australia, and Malbec Rosé from Argentina.

Rosé should be drunk as a young, juicy, fresh wine. The best examples exhibit flavours of ripe red fruits, but with crisp acidity. They are often good choices to accompany Indian food, salmon fillet and cold meats. Rosé offers a freshness that makes it an ideal drink on a hot day.

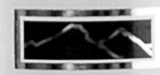

PRODUCE OF FRANCE

MONTAGNE NOIRE

GRENACHE ROSÉ

VIN DE PAYS D'OC

MIS EN BOUTEILLE PAR LES PRODUCTEURS REUNIS
FONCALIEU - 11290 ARZENS - FRANCE

Champagne
&
Sparkling
Wines

Putting the bubbles into wine can be done in several ways but only sparkling wines made in a certain region of northern France can be called Champagne.

The sediment, or lees, left behind by the spent yeast stays in contact with the wine until dégorgement, and imparts biscuity flavours and complexity.

Dégorgement

'Dégorgement' is the removal of the lees, in order to render the wine clear and bright. A process known as 'rémuge', which involves the twisting and turning of the bottles, slowly shifts the lees to the neck of the bottle. The necks of the bottles are then passed through a solution of freezing brine in order to freeze the first inch or so of wine now containing the lees. When the cap is removed, the pressure in the bottle forces out the ice pellet.

To finish, the wine lost during 'dégorgement' is replaced by a mixture of wine and cane sugar, called the 'dosage' or 'Liqueur d'Expedition'. The amount of sugar added has a bearing on the final style of the wine, for example a small amount of sugar is added for the dryish style of Brut while more is added for the quite sweet and sticky rich.

The best way to produce sparkling wine is the 'Methode Traditionelle', practised in Champagne and elsewhere. Base wines high in acidity and fermented to dryness are bottled and a small amount of sugar and yeast is then introduced to create a second fermentation. It is the second fermentation which creates carbon dioxide and thus the bubbles which give the wine its sparkle. As the carbon dioxide is unable to escape into the air it dissolves into the wine.

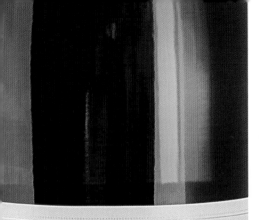

A cheaper form of secondary fermentation can take place in closed tanks. Known as 'Cuve close', the wine is bottled under pressure so that it retains carbon dioxide. This method is generally reserved for less expensive fizz.

Particular grape varieties are sought the world over. Chardonnay and Pinot Noir both have the attributes required to make great champagnes and sparkling wines. Although the best champagne may be a first choice for many as a 'desert island' bottle, there are plenty of fine sparkling wines around.

Where in the World?

Areas of England with chalky soil, combined with the country's cool climate, make it capable of producing top-quality sparkling wine. Fruity and expressive sparklers come from riper fruit in countries such as Australia, USA, New Zealand and South Africa, while the favoured choice from Spain is Cava, a lighter sparkling wine made from indigenous grape varieties.

Fortified
Wines

Fortified wines are wines which have had extra alcohol added during their production. Sherry is fortified after the juice has fermented to the extent that all the sugar has been used up. In the case of port, fortification takes place during fermentation.

Sherry

Sherry is the unique wine made in southwest Spain. Like Champagne, its name is protected by law and may only be applied to the wines made in the 'Sherry Triangle' around the town of Jerez.

'White, chalky' Albariza soil, ample sunshine and the cool influence of the Atlantic Ocean help to ripen the Palomino grapes which produce the base wine for sherry. The best sweetening wine will be made from the Pedro Ximénez grape.

After fortification, the sherry will be stored in casks (butts), until the following year, when classification will take place. All sherry butts are filled just five-sixths full. The delicate wines, fortified to a maximum of 15.5 per cent alcohol, will be classified as finos. There are three major styles of fino: fino, manzanilla and amontillado. The type of fino depends on the influence of flor, a yeast unique to Jerez. It's in the atmosphere and grows on the surface of the wine, affecting its composition and flavour. The very presence of flor produces the characteristic tangy and 'yeasty' nose and flavour of the dry sherries.

Butts not classified as finos will develop into the richer wines known as olorosos, which are fortified to 18 per cent alcohol, a level too high to be affected by flor. Olorosos mature in direct contact with air and are sometimes sweetened during this process.

To maintain style and consistency, a system of fractional blending and maturation takes place. Known as the solera system, this allows a younger wine to be added to an older wine after one-third of the older wine has been drawn off for bottling.

Styles of Sherry

Sherry is diverse and therefore not only makes an excellent aperitif wine, but is also extremely versatile with food:

FINO: light and dry

MANZANILLA: delicate, dry with a salty tang

OLOROSO: full, smooth with a walnut flavour

AMONTILLADO: dry, smooth, nutty

PALO CORTADO: amontillado nose, oloroso-like palate

PALE CREAM: crisp, subtle sweetness

CREAM: sweet, dried fruit flavour

PEDRO XIMÉNEZ: rich, sweet, raisin-like flavour

Port

Port is made in various styles in the Douro Valley, a rugged, yet beautiful and stunning location in northern Portugal. The area was first demarcated in 1756.

A rich, fortified wine, port is made by stopping the fermentation before it is complete, in order to arrest or keep some residual sugar in the wine. In most cases, maturation takes place in Villa Nova de Gaia, close to the coolness of the mouth of the River Douro and opposite the city of Oporto.

The steep slopes alongside the River Douro and its tributaries are terraced to accommodate the vines. Labour therefore is still pretty intensive and most of the picking is done by hand. Over forty different grape varieties are grown here, but only five have been identified as ideal for the production of port: Touriga Nacional, Touriga Francesa, Tinta Barroca, Tinta Roriz, and Tinto Cão.

Once the ripe grapes are picked, fermentation will follow in stainless steel tanks, although some 'quintas' (vineyards) still tread grapes in 'lagares', open-top granite tanks. Ordinary port will often have a long maturation in casks, known as pipes, or in large wooden vats, while vintage port will develop for most of its life in bottle.

Styles of Port

Although port is seen as an after-dinner drink or a classic accompaniment to cheese, particularly Stilton, its breadth of styles means that it can be suitable with a range of food. A sweet tawny port for instance, works beautifully with a rich pâté.

WHITE PORT: made from white grapes. Dry or sweet.

RUBY: youthful, spicy, fruity, and with a deep ruby colour.

VINTAGE CHARACTER: deeply coloured, full-bodied port around four years of age (blended).

TAWNY: aged in wood, tawny coloured, smooth, and with flavours of dried fruits. A blend of grapes from several harvests, an indication of age (10, 20, 30 or 40 years old) will be shown on the label of the best ports.

COLHEITA: a single harvest Tawny. At least seven years old, having rich, smooth, complex 'Tawny' characteristics.

LATE BOTTLED VINTAGE (LBV): port from a good year (not necessarily a 'declared' vintage). Matured in wood for five or six years. Accessible, more complex than ruby or vintage character.

SINGLE QUINTA: single harvest, from an individual vineyard. Maturing in bottle to reveal black fruits and spice on the palate. Throws sediment (crust), so needs decanting.

VINTAGE: single exceptional harvest, which may be declared. Aged for two to three years in wood, then slowly in bottle, for up to three decades. Complex, blackberry-like flavours, spicy and powerful in youth. Needs decanting.

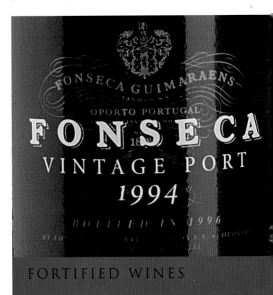

FORTIFIED WINES

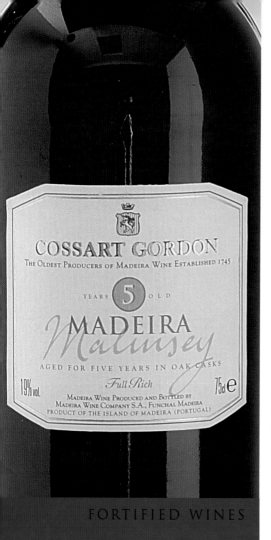

Madeira

Madeira is a small, mountainous island in the Atlantic Ocean. Lying 350 miles from the coast of Morocco, the island is warm and temperate the whole year round, and has fertile, volcanic soil.

Due to its location, Madeira was once a port of call for sailing ships bound for the Americas. Even today, North America is still an important market. The Madeira vines cling to steep, terraced vineyards in coastal settings at high altitude.

Since 1993, it has been compulsory for the best Madeiras, labelled Sercial, Verdelho, Bual or Malmsey, to be made from a minimum of 85 per cent of the named variety. Those called seco (dry), meio seco (medium dry), meio doce (medium rich) or doce (rich/sweet), are made from the chameleon Tinta Negra Mole grape, which has the knack of imitating the four 'classic' varieties.

Manufacture

Madeira can be made in the same method as port (by stopping fermentation) or, to produce the sweeter wines, by blending in the same manner applied to sherry.

The young wine is then put through a process unique to Madeira, called 'Estufagem'. In the days of sailing ships, casks of Madeira were shipped as ballast. During the slow voyage to the Indies and back, the wine was gradually warmed up and then cooled down. The character of the wine would change, developing a softness and toffee-like texture.

A heated-tank ('estufas') system recreates those conditions, by slowing heating and cooling the wines in a hot store. After Estufagem, the wines mature, before being blended, sometimes in a solera system.

Portugal's Madeira is a hidden gem of a wine, capable of ageing fantastically. Even when opened, the sweet styles will not really change, allowing the consumer to enjoy the drink over a period of time, if the bottle lasts that long!

FORTIFIED WINES

Key

Main wine-producing areas of the world

United States

Europe

Argentina

Chile

Uruguay

South Africa

Australia

New Zealand

Wines by Country

A quick glance at the shelves in a supermarket would make anyone think that wine was made all over the world.

However, this is not the case as grapes require warmth and water in order to thrive. Of course, there are many other factors affecting the final quality of a wine.

Different countries, and indeed different regions, have acquired reputations for certain types of wine. For years, France was regarded as the true home of quality wine but now Australian and Californian vintages are among the best regarded.

Champagne

▲ PARIS

Alsace

FRANCE

Burgundy

Jura

Loire Valley

Key

Main wine-producing
areas of France

Bordeaux

Geneva

Lyon

Savoie

Rhône
Valley

Provence

Languedoc
Roussillon

WINES BY COUNTRY

France

France still sets the standards by which most of the world's finest wines are judged, but as far as store sales are concerned, Australian wines are rapidly moving into pole position.

In contrast though, pick up almost any international wine list in a restaurant and French wines still dominate. It will be fascinating to see if French wines can fight back over the next decade.

Categorisation

The system of Appellations d'Origine Contrôlées (AC) used in France – which defines the region in which a wine's grapes are grown, the varieties used, and the manner of production – may have its restrictions but it is still the first piece of information many people look for on a label. Vin de Pays, the lowest category of French wine, does not follow strict AC rules, but today it can hold many a pleasant surprise and bargain for the wine lover.

59

PRODUCE OF FRANCE

MIS EN BOUTEILLE AU CHATEAU

GRAND VIN
DE
CHATEAU LATOUR
PREMIER GRAND CRU CLASSÉ
PAUILLAC
1997   750 ml

APPELLATION PAUILLAC CONTRÔLÉE

Bordeaux

In terms of producing fine wines Bordeaux is the largest and most important region of France. Throughout its long history Bordeaux has had connections with England, and during a 300-year spell from 1152, was under English rule. In many ways, the British wine trade developed around Claret.

Bordeaux lies on the rivers Garonne and Dordogne, which join to become the Gironde, before flowing into the Atlantic. The climate, influenced by the sea and rivers, is mild, slightly humid and summers tend to be long and warm.

The soil in Bordeaux is generally gravel, clay or sand and limestone. Gravel's warm and well-draining properties suit Cabernet Sauvignon, and can be found in the Haut-Médoc, while the clay and limestone soil of St Émilion and Pomerol is preferable for Merlot and Cabernet Franc. The Petit Verdot grape adds 'seasoning' to the wines of the Médoc and Graves (Left Bank), while Malbec contributes colour and fruitiness in both Left Bank and Right Bank wines, such as those from the Côtes de Bourg. These grape varieties are blended together in varying percentages from château to château, to make Bordeaux red wines.

Bordeaux Wines

The white wines of Bordeaux are made from three main varieties of grape: Sémillon, Sauvignon Blanc, and Muscadelle, with some Colombard and Ugni Blanc being incorporated into the lesser wines. Sémillon's lemon characteristics and relatively high alcohol content make it a popular choice for both dry and sweet dessert wines. Lowish in acidity, it's often blended with the early ripening Sauvignon, which is lively both in aromatics and acidity. Muscadelle adds a certain peachy, musky, and floral quality. Bordeaux also produces Rosé and Claret.

Bordeaux's most famous red wines are the classified first growths, Cru Classé of the Médoc, such as Château Latour, and the Merlot-dominated wines of St Émilion and Pomerol, such as Château Cheval-Blanc and Château Petrus. Outstanding dry whites include Château Carbonnieux, but it is the sweet wines of Sauternes, which are probably better known, such as the first growth of Château d'Yquem.

Did You Know?

Red wine production accounts for around 85 per cent of the total Bordeaux wine production. Bordeaux grows a small amount of the white Merlot, as opposed to the famous Merlot Noir grape.

Burgundy

The hallowed ground of Burgundy is home to the greatest Chardonnays and Pinot Noirs in the world. Sadly though, in recent years not all of the wines made here have met the standards of their predecessors. Having said that, there are some smart, up-and-coming young producers around and today Burgundy finds itself on a bit of a roll.

Burgundy was one of the first French regions to be known for its wine outside its boundaries. Favoured by kings and queens, the much sought-after wines of Burgundy were also a passion for Thomas Jefferson.

Situated in central France, Burgundy stretches from Dijon in the north, to just south of Macon in the south. The districts of Chablis, sixty miles to the northwest of Dijon, and Beaujolais, to the south of Mâcon, are both considered part of the region. Due to the influence of the church and the French law of inheritance, the vineyards of Burgundy are very fragmented.

Therefore the 'négociant' (the merchant who buys direct from the grower) has an important role in the making and selling of the wines. 'Domaine' (estate) bottled Burgundy is a direct reflection of an individual grower, who often tends the vines, makes the wine, and bottles it.

Burgundy Grapes

Chardonnay is the principal white grape suited to the calcareous/limestone soil of Burgundy. White Burgundy combines power and elegance but early maturing wines are also produced, along with the racy, cool climate white wines of Chablis.

The Aligoté grape is also planted. This makes crisp and lively white wines and is the classical base for Kir. Pinot Blanc and Sauvignon Blanc are also planted in small quantities. The major black variety in the region is Pinot Noir, except in Beaujolais where Gamay reigns supreme. In Burgundy, Pinot Noir is capable of producing wines of exceptional class, elegance and ability to age. It's a difficult customer though and great care is required to grow and vinify this grape. Gamay on the other hand, provides colour, lots of fruit and acidity in Beaujolais and is also used in the Mâconnais.

The most famous and expensive wines of Burgundy include those of the Domaine de la Romanée Conti, Domaine Leflaive and Lafon.

Alsace

Alsace with its villages, vineyards and towns lining the foothills of the Vosges mountains, is one of the most picturesque wine regions of France. This unique area of northeast France, which produces some of the greatest white wines in the country, still prides itself on making handcrafted wines and steers clear of outside investment.

The region's continental climate is exceptionally dry. Almost all Alsace wines are white and dry, with the exception of late harvest wines and some red wine produced from Pinot Noir. The soil is extremely varied, with the best vineyards classified as Grand Cru.

Alsace Grapes

Mostly grapes of Germanic origin are grown here, but the resulting wines are much more expressive and fuller-bodied than those over the border. Often consumed with food, the main grape varieties, which are always mentioned on

the label, are Gewürztraminer, Riesling, Tokay-Pinot-Gris, Muscat, Pinot Blanc, and Sylvaner.

Some of the greatest wines of Alsace are the Vendange Tardives and Sélection des Grains Nobles, which can live for over forty years. Outstanding wines include: Riesling Clos Ste., Hune from F.E. Trimbach, Domaine Zind Humbrecht's Gewürztraminer Rangen Grand Cru, and Hugel's Riesling Vendage Tardive.

> ### *Did You Know?*
> *Alsace has the most complex geological make-up of all the great wine regions of France.*

Produit Français

« Ce vin du Viennois

à odeur de violette »
(Pline le Jeune)

CÔTE - RÔTIE

CÔTE BLONDE

APPELLATION CÔTE-RÔTIE CONTRÔLÉE

R. ROSTAING, Propriétaire à Ampuis (Rhône) FRANCE

Mis en bouteille à la propriété

FRANCE

The Rhône

The Rhône Valley is one of the oldest wine-producing regions of France. There is evidence of wine production taking place here as long ago as 600 BC.

The wine region of the Rhône Valley starts just south of Vienne, the gateway to the northern Rhône, where the only permitted black grape variety is Syrah. The southern Rhône, where the Grenache grape variety takes centre stage, lies south of Montelimar and extends to Avignon. More often than not, the Grenache will be blended with other grapes, such as Carignan, Cinsault and Mourvèdre.

Hand harvesting takes place in many of the terraced vineyards in the narrow northern Rhône Valley. Vines are often trained on ingenious supports, so that they can withstand the powerful Mistral wind which blows down the valley.

Planted on mostly granite and sandstone soils, Syrah produces full-bodied wines, which have high tannin content when young and therefore age very well. Côte Rôtie, one of the great wines of France, can mix power and elegance and is often a blend of Syrah and the white grape Viognier.

Hermitage

Hermitage is not only the most recognised name associated with Syrah, but also an appellation making wines of great depth, concentration and structure which are capable of ageing over decades in bottle. Crozes-Hermitage and St. Joseph are generally lighter, while the very best vineyards from Cornas, with their attractive 'rustic' edge, make wines which at best rival those from Hermitage.

The white wines of the northern Rhône are predominantly made from Viognier, Marsanne and Roussanne. In Condrieu, Viognier is used to make distinctive peach and apricot-flavoured wines, with high alcohol and ample body. Marsanne and Roussanne are often blended together to make the dramatic white wines of Hermitage and other neighbouring appellations.

The world-famous wines of Châteauneuf-du-Pape are produced in the southern Rhône, where up to thirteen different grape varieties are permitted in the blend! The wines of Gigondas and Vacqueyras often represent great value and possess similar characteristics to the best Chateauneufs, while Tavel is home to the dry and full-bodied rosé.

Most generic Côtes du Rhône, along with Côtes du Rhône Villages, come from the Southern Rhône. The latter, which can include the name of the village, such as Visan, can be another source of well-priced wines.

Did You Know?

Château Grillet is a single estate appellation, making wines from Viognier.

Pope John XXII died in 1334, only a year after his new palace (Châteauneuf-du-Pape) was complete.

The Loire Valley

In comparison to the rest of France, the Loire has a cool climate. The area is capable of producing a wide range of wines, from light, dry, and crisp whites, to rosé, medium-bodied reds, and luscious dessert wines.

It is also a region where extremely good sparkling wines are made. It was not until the mid 1940s that the Loire's wines began to gain a reputation outside their local markets but since then, the region's white wines, in particular, have featured on many restaurant wine lists.

FRANCE

The Loire is the longest river in France and provides an entry to four main wine areas which lie between the Atlantic and the centre of France. Around Nantes (Muscadet country), the influence of the sea is evident, while inland, the so-called central vineyards, including Sancerre and Pouilly-Fumé, have a continental climate. Anjou-Saumur and Touraine lie between these two extremes. The vast size of the region means that there are many different soil types, but chalk and clay are the most prominent.

The most important grape varieties are Muscadet, Chenin Blanc and Sauvignon Blanc for white wines, and Cabernet Franc for red wines, with a little Pinot Noir grown in and around Sancerre. Muscadet, is a dry, fresh and crisp white wine, and a seafood wine 'par excellence'. The term 'sur lie', usually associated with better-quality Muscadet, indicates that the wine has spent time maturing on the lees and is bottled directly, to give added concentration and a faint prickle of carbon dioxide.

In Anjou-Saumur, mostly dry or medium sweet white wines are produced from the Chenin Blanc grape. As well as having a bearing on the wines, the local chalk soil (known as 'Tufa') is evident in the extraordinary buildings typical of the area, where the white stone has a striking effect.

Many of the sweet wines come from the sheltered area around the river Layon, a tributary of the Loire and are affected by noble rot. They are some of the hidden gems of the wine world and, like many of the white wines made from the Chenin Blanc, can age amazingly well.

The best red wines of the Loire are made from the Cabernet Franc grape, in the subdistrict of Touraine. Generally medium-bodied, these delicious and elegant wines are made to drink young, but can also surprise with mid-term cellaring. Chinon, Bourgueil, Saint Nicholas de Bourgueil and Saumur Champigny are four appellations to look out for. Frustratingly, there's some variation with the quality of wines from Vouvray and Montlouis but the best white wines are magnificent expressions of the Chenin Blanc grape.

Sancerre wine takes its name from the hilltop town of the area. The district's wines are arguably the world's most famous appellation connected to the tangy, piquant wines made from the Sauvignon Blanc grape. Across the river Loire and just a few miles away, is Pouilly Sur Loire, home to Pouilly-Fumé, where the white wines are produced from Sauvignon. Tending to be a little sterner, they are very good with food. Due to its proximity to the top end of Burgundy, the red wines of the central vineyards are made from the Pinot Noir grape. Look out too, for the wines of Quincy, Reuilly, and Menetou Salon.

Did You Know?

Many of the white wines of the Loire Valley age remarkably well, changing in character from the mineral, flintlike flavours of youth to an almost honey-and-apricot textured complexity. Even 50–60-year-old wines can be in perfect shape!

FRANCE

Languedoc-Roussillon & Provence

Languedoc-Roussillon is a large area that sweeps across southern France from the Spanish border to the Rhône estuary. Commonly known as the Midi, it produces almost one third of all French wines and is currently a hot bed of innovation and exciting winemaking.

Hillside locations are replacing the flatland vineyards which once produced an enormous amount of Vin Ordinaire. Emphasis is now being placed on lower yields, barrique (a wooden barrel associated with Burgundy) ageing and more complex blending.

Many Rhône varieties, such as Syrah and Grenache, are planted here to grow alongside Cabernet Sauvignon, Merlot and Chardonnay. Other well-known grape varieties can be seen on wine labels, particularly from the Vin de Pay d'Oc, an area covering the whole of the Languedoc-Roussillon. Important appellations include Minervois, Corbières, Fitou and Côtes du Roussillon.

Up and Coming

Provence lies to the southeast of Avignon and extends to the Italian border. A popular holiday destination, mostly dry rosé and red wines are made here. With a Mediterranean climate and some favourable soil conditions, both Languedoc-Roussillon and Provence can provide consistency in terms of quality against price, without too much variation from one year to the next.

Several Australian winemakers have now brought their own ideas and experience to

> ### Did You Know?
> *The wines of Maury, with flavours of sweet blackberry and a nutty, raisin-like richness, make an excellent partner to chocolate.*

this part of France, which is sometimes described as 'where the new world meets the old'. Dynamic and forward thinking, they are shaping the future of these two historic regions. It is interesting to note that well-known French companies looking to expand their interests have also established wineries and contracts with local growers.

Some producers, such as Mas de Daumas Gassac, have successfully made and sold wines under a humble Vin de Pays, while reaching a level of quality and price that one would normally associate with more famous place names. Gradually, the south of France is no longer being seen as the bargain basement of bulk wine!

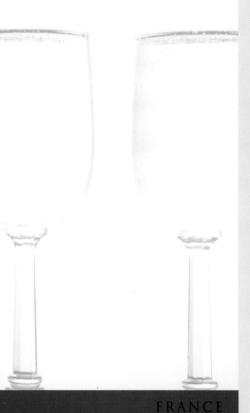

Champagne

The Champagne district is the most northerly wine region of France, located some ninety miles northeast of Paris. The method of production for champagne is explained on pages 44–47.

Originally, the wines of Champagne were still. The cellar master at the Abbey of Hautvillers, a certain Pierre Pérignon (1639–1715), developed a system of blending, whereby the wines from different areas in Champagne and made from different grape varieties, were blended together.

Although Dom Pérignon has been credited as being the inventor of sparkling Champagne, there is little real evidence to support this. There are claims that it was the English who put the sparkle into imported Champagne wines, in the seventeenth century. One school of thought argues that warm weather caused the wine to undergo a secondary fermentation in the barrels in which it was exported.

Champagne Grapes

The region of Champagne has a marginal climate and a unique form of chalk soil covered by a thin layer of richer top soil. Three important grape varieties are grown – Pinot Noir, Pinot Meunier and Chardonnay. The majority of the vines are planted in the Montagne de Reims (Pinot Noir), Vallée de la Marne (Pinot Noir and Pinot Meunier), Côte des Blancs (Chardonnay), Côte de Sezanne and Aube (Pinot Noir).

Champagne is a protected name. Only sparkling wines from this region made by the Champagne method are allowed to carry the name on the label.

Germany

Some of the greatest white wines in the world come from Germany. When made from the Riesling grape, by a well-respected grower, German wines can be extremely complex and deliver immense satisfaction.

Key

Main wine-producing areas of Germany

BERLIN ▲

GERMANY

AHR

FRANKFURT ▲

Mosel-Saar-Ruwer

Nahe

Rheinhessen

Hessische-Bergstrasse

Franken

Pfalz

STUTTGART ▲

Württemberg

Baden

WINES BY COUNTRY

The cool climate is just one of the factors explaining why German wines are some of the most difficult to make. Several of the vineyards lie at the northern limit for wine production. Nonetheless, in good years the grapes ripen slowly and can provide a wonderful balance between fruit and acidity.

Winemaking was introduced to the region by the Romans who observed where the snow first melted, indicating where grapes might successfully ripen.

A grading system evolved, which linked quality to grape ripeness, rather than vineyard location. This notion has been challenged by several respected growers, who argue that precise location is equally important. Traditionally, QMP (Qualitätswein mit Prädikat) wines, are made without chaptalisation (the addition of sugar prior to fermentation) and are categorised depending on the degree of natural grape sugar at the time of harvest.

The categories are as follows:

KABINETT: very light and perfect as an aperitif.

SPÄTLESE: distinctly off-dry.

AUSLESE: much sweeter, with some noble rot apparent in some cases.

BEERENAUSLESE (BA): rich, intense, sweet wines.

TROCKENBEERENAUSLESE (TBA): made from individual handpicked berries, 100 per cent noble rot. The richest wines, at best balanced with crisp acidity.

EISWEIN: picked at BA ripeness or above when frozen. Sweet, intense and with pinpoint acidity.

Regions

Two new generic labelling terms have been introduced: 'Classic' and 'Selection'. Linked to dry wines made from traditional grapes, 'selection' indicates that the wine comes from an individual vineyard in one specified region.

Germany's wine regions of note include Mosel-Saar-Ruwer, Rheingau, Nahe and Pfalz. The steep, south-facing vineyards of Mosel-Saar-Ruwer overlook the River Mosel and its tributaries, the Saar and the

Ruwer. Slate soil is important here. Mosel wines, traditionally sold in tall, green bottles, are pale in colour, light in body, with racy acidity and elegance.

Rheingau wines are fuller in style, with the river Rhine being influential. The vineyards, such as the Rüdesheimer Berg, are also angled steeply. Halfway in style between a Mosel and a Rhein, Nahe wines are fresh, clean and sometimes 'minerally'.

Wines from the Pfalz region are growing in popularity. Pfalz has the warmest climate of Germany's wine-growing regions and is home to some of Germany's most innovative winemakers and some exciting wines. Certain wines, such as those from the Lingenfleder estate, excel. However, Pfalz is also home to a great deal of Liebfraumilch production.

Did You Know?
Top-quality estate wines from Germany once fetched higher prices than first-growth Bordeaux!

MOSEL - SAAR - RUWER

SELBACH

2001
PIESPORTER GOLDTRÖPFCHEN
RIESLING KABINETT

QUALITÄTSWEIN MIT PRÄDIKAT
ERZEUGER J. & H. SELBACH, WEINKELLEREI, D-54492 ZELTINGEN/MOSEL
L. A. P. NR. 2 606 365 026 02

Italy

Italy has a million grape growers, hundreds of grape varieties, and an amazing number of wine regions and styles.

MILAN ▲

ITALY

Friuli-Venezia
Guilia

VENICE ▲

Veneto

Key

Main wine-producing areas of Italy

Tuscany

ROME ▲

Lazio

Puglia

SARDINIA

SICILY

Arguably, the country provides greater diversity than any other wine-producing nation. Native grape varieties are still Italy's strength, but some notable success has also been achieved with international grape varieties, such as Cabernet Sauvignon, Merlot, Syrah, and Chardonnay.

Categorisation

Italian wines tend to be best appreciated with food. This is a nation where regional food and wines are enjoyed together, a natural evolution that has developed over centuries. Cultivation of the vine was introduced by both the Greeks and the Etruscans. The Greeks named Italy 'Oenotria', land of the vine.

Although Italy's wine laws have come in for some criticism, they broadly follow the French model, with DOCG (Denominazione Origine Controllata e Garantita) being reserved for a few 'top' wines, which are subject to strict rules of control. DOC (Denominazione di Origine Controllata), introduced in 1963, guarantees that the wine has been produced in the named vineyard area (e.g. Valpolicella DOC).

Methods of production are also specified. The newest category is IGT (Indicazione Geographica Tipica), which mirrors the

French Vin de Pays. The removal of restrictions has led to winemakers making the most of blending opportunities and at best, making truly exciting and innovative wines. Vino da Tavola (table wine) represents not only the simplest wines, but also super-premium and expensive wines made from non-indigenous grape varieties, such as Sassicaia, a pioneering Cabernet produced in Tuscany, which was promoted to a special sub-zone status in the Bolgheri (DOC) in 1994.

Italy's climate tends to be more consistent than northern France's but there is quite a variation from north to south. The best grape varieties, in terms of the quality of the wines produced, are Nebbiolo (northwest Italy, Piedmont), which reaches its greatest heights in Barolo and Barbaresco, both of which are DOCGs. In central Italy, the principal grape in Chianti DOCG is Sangiovese, which in its various clones also appears in Brunello di Montalcino (DOCG) and Vino Nobile di Montepulciano (DOCG). This trio make up some of Tuscany's most impressive wines.

Best Whites

Veneto, home to Valpolicella and Soave, is found in the north. Some of Italy's best white wines are produced in Trentino and Friuli, in what is often referred to as the varietal northeast. The south has made great strides in improving its wines, and evidence of success can be seen in wines such as Salice Salentino (DOC) from Apulia.

ITALY

Rioja

Duero

MADRID
▲

PORTUGAL

SPAIN

Cádiz

Valdepeñas

Malaga

Sherry

Key

Main wine-producing areas
of Spain and Portugal

Spain & Portugal

In recent years there has been major investment in Spanish vineyards and wineries, and the country's best wines are now world class. Its reputation has been carved by red wines, particularly those from Rioja.

Several growers have identified and recognised the importance of old vines, and today these are partly responsible for the super-concentrated and very expensive premium reds.

SPAIN

Spain has more land under vine than any other country. The most important Spanish variety is Tempranillo, closely followed by Garnacha. For white wines, Viura and the 'workhorse' Airén are grown widely, with the fashionable Albariño taking centre stage in Rías Baixas. Not surprisingly, Chardonnay, Cabernet Sauvignon, and Merlot are planted in the majority of Spanish wine regions, except Rioja.

The best Spanish wines are quality graded at DO (Denominacionde Origen), the equivalent of the French AC, and DOCa, a higher-quality grade introduced in 1991, initially for the wines of Rioja. Although DOCa applies only to Rioja, regions such as Ribera del Duero, Navarra, Penedes and Priorato are also producing some excellent wines.

Rioja

In Rioja the wines are made in three distinct sub-regions: Rioja Alavesa, Rioja Alta in the highlands and the hot and dry Rioja Baja. Rioja styles include Joven (young and unoaked), Crianza (twelve months in oak, released in the third year after the vintage), Reserva (one year minimum in barrels and two years in bottle or barrica combined, released in the fourth year after vintage) and Gran Reserva (minimum two years in barrels and three in bottle, may be released in their sixth year) which is produced in the very best years.

Ribera del Duero, situated at high altitude, is purely a red wine area. It is home to some of Spain's most sought-after and expensive wines made from the

Tempranillo grape, locally known as Tinta Fino.

Navarra, a neighbouring region to Rioja, is home to experimentation with Cabernet Sauvignon and Merlot often blended with indigenous grapes such as Garnacha and Tempranillo.

Spanish and international grapes are planted in the Mediterranean climate of Penedes. Many of the best Cava vineyards are found in this region.

Mostly red wines from Garnacha and Cariñena are grown in the mountainous setting of Priorato. These high-quality, structured wines can be truly exciting!

PORTUGAL

Portugal is a country concentrating on its amazing range of indigenous grape varieties, especially Touriga Nacional, Tinta Roriz, Trincadeira and Periquita. The regions of the Douro, Ribatejo, Alentejo, and Bairrada set the pace. For the wine consumer willing to try something different, Portugal can hold many a pleasant discovery.

United States

Although grapes are grown and wine is made in most American states, only in California and the Pacific northwest are grapes grown in significant quantities. Only wines from these areas have gained an international reputation for quality.

WASHINGTON STATE

OREGON

Napa Valley
SAN FRANCISCO

LOS ANGELES

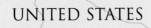

UNITED STATES

Key

▓

Main wine-producing areas
of the United States

CALIFORNIA

California's reputation has been built on bold, ripe, fruit-driven wines, which often carry their fair share of new oak. The state has had its problems, with almost every deadly wine disease rearing its ugly head at some stage, yet it has without doubt, some of the world's best growing conditions.

Regions

The Pacific Ocean is hugely influential, moderating a hot climate with its cool breezes and fogs. Most of California's commercial wines come from the warm and fertile Central Valley, but its premium wines tend to be made from fruit grown much closer to the coast.

The Napa Valley, sometimes referred to as the Bordeaux of California, is situated just north of San Francisco Bay. As an appellation (or AVA), Napa has a diversity of soil, climate, and topography, which particularly suits Cabernet Sauvignon and Merlot. A food culture has also evolved here, making it a destination for the rich and famous.

The areas of Sonoma and Carneros, separated from the Napa Valley by the Mayacamus Mountains, are much cooler and are therefore able to specialise in Pinot Noir and Chardonnay. Warmer districts, such as Dry Creek, are found in northern Sonoma, where some superb Zinfandels are produced. Zinfandel is California's 'own grape'. At best it produces blackberry-flavoured, full-bodied reds, often from old vines. At worst it also makes 'blush' or White Zin, a pale relation, bottled with a dash of sweetness.

The small, but up-and-coming Sierra Foothills area is a great source of Rhône and Italian varietals while south of San Francisco lies the region of Santa Cruz which is home to some top-class wineries.

PACIFIC NORTHWEST

Washington State and Oregon, collectively known as the Pacific northwest, like California lie on the western side of the country. Spanning three adjoining states, this is an area of rolling hills, rivers and valleys. Washington, with approximately 30,000 acres of vineyards, tends to be the warmer of the two regions. Its plantings focus mostly around the eastern side of the Cascade Mountain range.

Oregon, has only 12,000 acres of vineyards, which have developed in the cooler Willamette Valley. Burgundian and Alsatian grape varieties, such as Pinot Noir, Chardonnay, Pinot Gris and Muscat, thrive here. Oregon gained overnight fame in 1979 when David Lett of the Eyrie Vineyard entered the estate's 1975 Pinot Noir in a blind wine tasting competition, organised by the Burgundian négociant Robert Drouhin. Although Drouhin's Chambolle-Musigny 1959 came first, the Eyrie vineyard beat many famous Burgundy wines to come second. Oregon has been linked with Pinot Noir ever since.

Columbia Valley

Over the Columbia River in Eastern Washington, the dry and warm climate of the Columbia Valley is proving to be an excellent area to grow Cabernet Sauvignon, Merlot, Cabernet Franc and Syrah. Most of the vineyards here rely on irrigation, even though generally Washington tends to be quite wet.

The Columbia Valley maybe the best-known region, but the Walla Walla Valley is beginning to generate a great deal of excitement.

Argentina

Despite its economic problems Argentina is, undeniably, one of the world's most important wine-producing nations.

Mostly planted at high altitude, at the feet of the Andes mountains, vines benefit from long, warm, sunny days, and very cold nights. The melted snow from the mountains provides plenty of water to compensate for the low annual rainfall.

Not everything however, focuses on the Andes. From Salta in the north to Patagonia in the south, Argentina's northern and southernmost vineyards are 900 miles apart and the different regions produce wines with a distinct individuality.

Massive investment has taken place so the country's most progressive producers now have up-to-date equipment and facilities at their disposal. This investment has enabled the country's producers to concentrate on wines made at various price points, from the fruity and inexpensive, to the sophisticated wines of iconic status.

Regions

The three most significant wine-producing areas of Argentina are Mendoza, San Juan, and Rioja. The most significant wines exported from Argentina are the reds from Malbec and Cabernet Sauvignon, grown in Mendoza, where 75 per cent of the country's wines are produced. Aromatic white wines from the Torrontes grape variety also provide interest.

Malbec, which produces distinctive world-class wines, is the great trump card. Although very different to the Malbec you would find in France, the image of Argentina's winemaking is associated with this variety. Tempranillo, Barbera, Syrah, along with different styles of Bonarda and Sangiovese, can also provide some excellent wines.

Key

Main wine-producing areas
of Argentina and Uruguay

Uruguay

With a population of 3.2 million, Uruguay is a relatively small Latin American country. Sandwiched between Argentina, Brazil, and the Atlantic Ocean, Uruguay is as much European in culture, as it is South American.

Small, privately owned wineries make up the market, growing grape varieties that reflect the diverse culture.

Tannat

The grape varieties are mostly French in origin, although there is some influence from Spain and Italy. Tannat, a French variety, has been adapted as the "national grape." Introduced by Basque immigrants, Tannat has the potential to make full-bodied and characterful red wines, a different expression when compared to the traditional tannic wines from Madiran in southwest France.

Chile

Chile produces much less wine than Argentina, but has had greater success on the export markets. Known for its fruity and appealing wines, made from a wide range of grape varieties, Chile has the knack of producing wine styles that consumers are very happy to drink.

WINES BY COUNTRY

*Aconcagua
Valley*

*Casablanca
Valley*

SANTIAGO ▲

*Maipo
Valley*

*Rapel
Valley*

*Curicó
Valley*

*Maule
Valley*

CHILE

Key

Main wine-producing areas of Chile

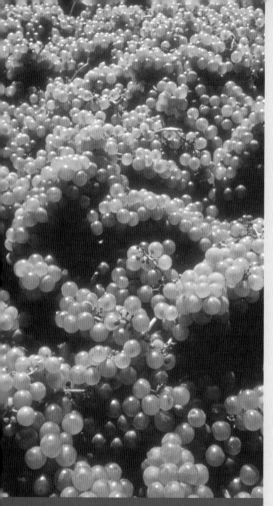

The foundations of today's Chilean wine industry were laid down in the 1850s. Many South Americans were great travellers and wealthy landowners made the long journey to visit the vineyards of Europe.

Carmenère

They returned with healthy vines from regions like Bordeaux, which explains the presence of Cabernet Sauvignon, Merlot and Carmenère, a grape variety that was, eventually, to give Chilean winemakers a real point of difference. It wasn't until the 1990s that Carmenère was identified by the French ampelographer Jean Michel Bourisiquot. Up until this time Carmenère had been growing among other vines and had been commonly mistaken for Merlot. Chilean Carmenère has abundant blackberry-like fruit, chocolate, and coffee flavours.

Chile has often been described as a viticultural paradise, with its dry summers and protection from the Pacific Ocean to the west and the mountains of the Andes to the east. Recognised as being phylloxera-free, Chile's vines have scarcely encountered any form of disease. The Atacama Desert to the north provides the final barrier.

Most of Chile's wine regions are found to the south of Santiago, with Aconcagua and Casablanca Valley to the north. Casablanca is particularly suited to growing white grapes, as the climate is strongly influenced by the cold Humboldt current off the Pacific Ocean.

The Central Valley region is a vast area which sits some 600 metres above sea level. There are four rivers which run from the Andes to the ocean, and each lends its name to an appellation. From north to south they are: Maipo Valley, Rapel, Curicó and Maule. Each area enjoys its own microclimate and has well-known sub-zones, such as Colchagua in Rapel, a source of some great Merlot.

International Acclaim

A high proportion of Chile's vineyards are planted with internationally popular classic grape varieties. Merlot helped Chilean wines to gain their reputation for the hallmark rich plummy characteristics that drinkers enjoy so much. Wines made from Cabernet Sauvignon were among the first to attract international acclaim, but by far the most interesting in terms of its history and potential is Carmenère.

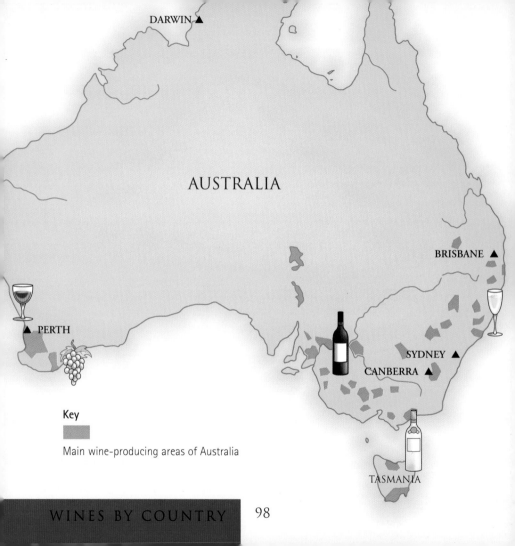

DARWIN ▲

AUSTRALIA

BRISBANE ▲

PERTH ▲

SYDNEY ▲

CANBERRA ▲

TASMANIA

Key

Main wine-producing areas of Australia

Australia

When it comes to technical know-how, the Australians are streets ahead of the pack. Wine was being commercially produced here as long ago as 1850 but in modern times Australia has become one of the most successful wine-producing countries in the world.

2000
WESTERN AUSTRALIA
SHIRAZ

At the top end of the market, an emphasis is being placed on more regional wines from places like Orange and Wrattonbully. Many of the new sites are in cooler areas, where the grapes provide better levels of natural acidity and aromatics. Australia built its reputation on wines showing ripe fruit flavours, often accompanied by noticeable use of oak, and in today's commercial middle ground, there's an enormous amount of wine being made to a standardised recipe, all backed up by full-throttle marketing.

Regions

The main wine-producing regions are near the cities of Perth in Western Australia, Adelaide in South Australia, Melbourne in Victoria, and Sydney in New South Wales. The climate tends to be hot, so irrigation is often necessary. The vast size of the country means that the states provide different growing conditions.

Some of Australia's most elegant wines are made in the relatively cool climate of Western Australia. White wines from the Chardonnay, Sémillon, Riesling, and Verdelho grapes have been successful, along with 'Bordeaux Blends' from Cabernet Sauvignon and Merlot.

South Australia includes the premium regions of the Barossa Valley, Coonawarra, and Adelaide Hills. Barossa Shiraz is world-famous for its inky, concentrated style, whilst Coonawarra, with its cooler climate and Terra Rossa soil, provides ideal conditions for some of Australia's outstanding Cabernet Sauvignon wines. The Adelaide Hills vineyards, situated at 450 metres above sea level, are proving to be a prime area for Riesling, Pinot Noir and bottle-fermented sparkling wines.

A great range of wines is produced in Victoria, including the unique liqueur Muscats. The Yarra Valley benefits from one of the coolest climates in Australia, resulting in fine Pinot Noirs, Rieslings, Chardonnays, and Cabernet Sauvignons. Australia's ultimate cool climate location however, is Tasmania. The island is home to some of the very best Pinot Noirs.

Hunter Valley

In New South Wales, the lower and upper Hunter Valley, located north of Sydney, has established itself as an area of 'classic' wines such as Sémillon and Shiraz. Both of these can develop with bottle age. The area of Orange is rapidly becoming known for its excellent cool climate wines while the Murrumbidgee Irrigation Area (MIA), which produces mostly commercial blends but with a smattering of extremely good botrytised wines, makes ten per cent of all Australian wine.

101 AUSTRALIA

Key

Main wine-producing areas of New Zealand

▲ AUCKLAND

Napier

▲ WELLINGTON

Blenheim

NEW ZEALAND

▲ CHRISTCHURCH

Queenstown

▲ DUNEDIN

New Zealand

With new wineries coming on stream at an amazing rate, New Zealand seems to raise the standard year on year.

Dramatic improvements have been made with red wines, with Pinot Noir all the rage. The total area under vine in New Zealand has more than doubled since 1990, and its wine industry is one of the most forward-thinking in the world.

Varieties

New Zealand wine is exciting because of the number of wines being produced from slightly less predictable grape varieties. Pinot Gris, Gewürztraminer and Riesling perform well while beyond Pinot Noir, it may be surprising to find Syrah, Zinfandel and even Pinotage producing the goods and joining Cabernet Sauvignon, Cabernet Franc, and Merlot.

New Zealand's wine-producing regions stretch from Auckland on the North Island to Central Otago, the country's most southerly wine region on South Island. The country benefits from a temperate, maritime climate and a wide range of wine styles are produced.

On the North Island some of New Zealand's top Cabernet-based reds are made in the Auckland/Henderson area. Waiheke Island, a short ferry journey from Auckland, enjoys a warm microclimate, which helps it to produce rich Bordeaux blends. In Northland, a number of boutique wineries are making high-class Cabernet-based reds and Chardonnay. Gisborne is Chardonnay country but also produces some promising Gewürztraminer.

Regions

Hawke's Bay is a region with a range of soils, including the Gimblett gravels, a 2,000-acre area of deep, stony soil. Full, rich Cabernet Sauvignon, Cabernet Franc and Merlot blends are made in good vintages.

The Chardonnays are some of New Zealand's most powerful and Sauvignon Blanc tends to be more rounded than the Marlborough style, from South Island. On the southeastern tip of North Island, the tiny region of Martinborough, also known as Wairarapa, excels in fine Pinot Noir.

On the South Island, Marlborough, the largest wine region in New Zealand, has seen extensive expansion since the mid 1970s. The maritime climate and stony soils are perfect for Sauvignon Blanc, which has become synonymous with Marlborough. Distinctive Riesling, Chardonnay, Pinot Noir and sparkling wines are also made in this hugely fashionable region. Very slightly cooler than Marlborough, Nelson has been successful with aromatic whites while Canterbury, in the Waipara sub-region, is particularly promising. In the small, cool, scenic, mountainous region of Central Otago, Pinot Noir is the star, rivalling the best of Martinborough. Riesling and Pinot Gris also perform well here.

NEW ZEALAND

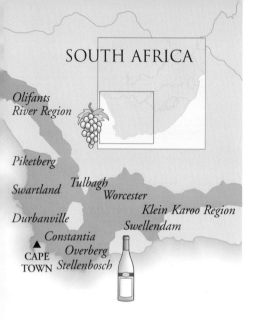

Olifants
River Region

Piketberg

Swartland Tulbagh
           Worcester

Durbanville   Klein Karoo Region
        Swellendam
   Constantia
      Overberg
CAPE Stellenbosch
TOWN

SOUTH AFRICA

Key

Main wine-producing areas
of South Africa

South Africa

**Today, South Africa has a
forward-looking and vibrant
wine industry that's making
up for lost time, fast!
Despite the fact that wine
has been made in South
Africa since 1659, it's only
over the past decade or
so that its strengths and
potential have been
discovered. South Africa's
best-known vine and wine is
Pinotage, bred by crossing
Pinot Noir and Cinsault.**

On paper, South Africa has everything to create great wines: a favourable climate, soil and an energetic band of talented winemakers. It's easy to find young winemakers who have travelled and worked in other wine-producing countries throughout the world, gaining valuable experience along the way.

The Cape and surrounding areas are cooled by the Atlantic Ocean, Indian Ocean and the Benguela current from Antarctica. The vineyards are mostly set in regions that enjoy some of the most spectacular scenery in the world. The varied topography creates diverse growing conditions and terroir, with some of the top wines expressing a true sense of place.

Regions

The best-known regions include Constantia, Paarl, Stellenbosch, Robertson, Swartland, and Malmesbury, Walker Bay, and Elgin. The cool, coastal setting of Constantia produces some top-quality dry and sweet white wines and Merlot shows great potential. Paarl includes the sub-region of Franschhoek, where Sauvignon and Sémillon perform particularly well. Paarl itself, is home to ripe, full-bodied and well-rounded wines.

Stellenbosch is the source of some of South Africa's finest red wines, from vineyards set in mountain foothills. Like the Napa Valley in California, you will find many good restaurants here too.

Robertson, 'The Valley of Vines and Roses', is set inland. A hot area irrigated from the Breede River, stony, lime-rich soils and cool evenings and nights help produce surprisingly good Chardonnay and Sauvignon Blanc. This is very much an up-and-coming region.

Swartland and Malmesbury, with its coastal location, is the source of some superbly balanced red wines. Walker Bay and Elgin meanwhile, is a cool and humid area southeast of Cape Town. Look out for some aromatic Sauvignon Blanc and Riesling from Elgin, and classy Pinot Noir and Chardonnay from Walker Bay.

Shopping for Wine

Shopping for wine can be quite a challenge, as there is often an immense range to choose from. Sometimes a little planning will be in your favour. Just knowing the type or style of a wine you want will make your buying decision that much easier.

Building up some knowledge of the various wine merchants, in your area and on the internet, can be very advantageous. Each merchant tends to have a particular strong point.

One may be extremely good on Bordeaux for example, or specialise in Italian wines, and they will be happy to pass on their experience to you – the customer.

Remember too, that some knowledge of which producers are making particularly good wine, or which regions offer good value, puts you in a much more secure position.

Bottles

There was a time when you could almost tell at an instant where a wine came from, just by looking at the shape of the bottle. This still holds true for some of the more traditional regions, such as Alsace or Bordeaux, but a glance or two around the shelves of your local supplier will also reveal the influence of design teams keen to catch the eye with bottle shapes that stand out from the crowd.

The Label

A wine label provides an excellent opportunity to send a message and pass on information to a potential customer.

In Europe, a place name may suffice. Chablis, Sancerre and Châteauneuf-du-Pape are all examples of French wines that can easily sell due to the fact that the name is recognised. In the 'New World' however, varietal labelling is the norm, as an increasing amount of wine is sold on the back of the name of the grape variety. The world's most popular grape, Chardonnay, could be perceived as a wine style, such is the influence carried by its name alone. The fact that most white Burgundy is made from Chardonnay is left for those of us who care to find out.

Depending on the wine, and in some cases the region, the name of the producer can be extremely important. You may wish to take note of the vintage. This is particularly important where grapes are grown in marginal climates. Each label will also indicate the percentage of alcohol by volume, which can range from 7–15 per cent.

FRENCH WINES

In General

- **Appellation contrôlée (AC)** – in theory the best-quality category of French wine, with regulations defining vineyard, soil, grape varieties, yields, and alcohol levels.

- **Clos** – an enclosed vineyard.

- **Cru** – literally 'growth', indicating a distinguished vineyard site in Burgundy or property in Bordeaux.

- **Vieilles Vignes** – old vines. Although unregulated, there can be a distinct bearing on quality. A Chablis Vieilles Vignes for example, may have added concentration of flavour.

Champagne

- **Blanc de blancs** – made from white grapes (Chardonnay only).

- **Blanc de noirs** – made from red grapes, vinified without skin contact.

- **Brut** – dry or dryish in style.

- **Demi-sec** – sweet.

- **Doux** – very sweet.

- **Vintage** – a blend from a single year, sold after at least three years ageing.

Alsace

- **Grand cru** – classified vineyard site.

- **Sélection de grains nobles** – wine made from botrytis-affected grapes.

- **Vendange Tardive** – 'late harvest'/ specially grown ripe grapes.

Bordeaux

- **Cru Bourgeois** – classification of châteaux in the Médoc and some of the best value-for-money wines.

- **Cru-classé/grand cru-classé/premier grand cru-classé** – 'classified growth', divided into five 'tables' in the Médoc, or from the classification systems of the Graves, Sauternes, or St Emilion.

- **In Bordeaux, the name of the château, or property, is all important.**

Burgundy

- **Domaine** – estate or vineyard holding, belonging to a grower or négociant.

- **Grand cru** – top or finest vineyard sites.

- **Premier cru** – second highest category of vineyard site.

- **In Burgundy, the name of the grower or négociant is extremely important.**

Loire

- **Sec** – dry.

- **Demi-sec** – medium to dry.

- **Moelleux** – medium sweet to sweet.

- **Sur Lie** – generally associated with Muscadet, sur lie indicates that the wine has been bottled directly from its lees, without being racked or filtered.

- **The Loire has a relatively cool climate, so take note of the vintage.**

Rhône

The best wines are often from a specified region, appellation or cru, i.e. Côte Rôtie. Côtes du Rhône Villages carries a higher reputation than the general appellation.

GERMANY

- **Trocken** – dry.

- **Halbtroken** – semi-dry. In Germany, the grower and grape variety is worth nothing.

- **Verband Deutscher Prädikatsweingüter e. V (VDP)** – group of estates whose members have agreed to a set of regulations.

ITALY

- **Amarone** – dry Passito wine from Valpolicella.

- **Classico** – heartland of a DOC zone, generally producing better wines.

- **Passito** – wine made from dried or semi-dried grapes.

- **Recioto** – sweet passito wine.

- **Riserva** – should be the best wines, from the better vintages, which are held back or aged for longer than normal.

- **Superiore** – wine with higher alcohol than usual.

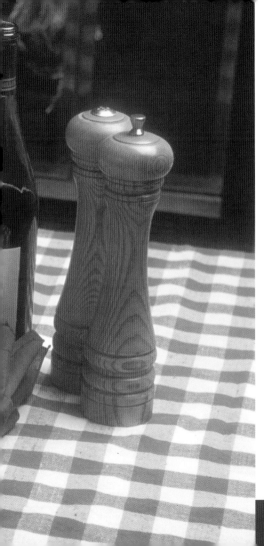

Pairing Food with Wine

Pairing wine with food does not have to be a science although it can be confusing, particularly today when there is such choice in the food and wine available.

Concentrating on the basic characteristics of various wines and the flavours of different foods is the key to finding compatibility. For a dinner party, it's well worth taking the trouble to select a wine which will show off your food to good effect.

When selecting a wine to accompany food, consider the main ingredient and, more importantly, the strongest flavour in the dish. It's easy to match chicken when it's plainly cooked, but in most cases a sauce or marinade provides the predominant flavour. A Thai green chicken curry presents a bit more of a challenge, but can be matched with a fruity Sémillon or Sauvignon Blanc. Sharply flavoured chutneys and spicy salsas can affect the taste of a wine, and if a dish is cooked in beer, it generally makes sense to drink a similar beverage with it.

In Restaurants

In a restaurant, you may be put on the spot, by having to choose a wine to drink with a combination of flavours and dishes. In these circumstances, look for food-friendly wines or bridging wines. Pinot Blanc, unoaked Chardonnay, and Pinot Gris from the white stable, and fruity reds such as Merlot and Pinot Noir, can be enjoyed with fish and lighter meat dishes. Rosés provide versatility and will go with a range of dishes, from salads to mildly spiced dishes.

DO'S AND DON'TS

The do's and don'ts of matching wines to food listed here are based on the flavour characteristics and profiles of the main wine styles. It is only a guideline as room should always be made for experimentation.

Fruit

✔ Serve dry fruity wines as aperitifs. Consider soft wines, e.g. Soave, with plain fish/white meats

✘ Overpower simple plain flavours in food

Aromatics

✔ Consider wines with aromatic characteristics with pronounced flavours in food

✘ Put pronounced wines, such as Sauvignon from New Zealand, with delicate fish dishes

Body and Alcohol

✔ Consider the balance and weight of the wine with the flavour of a dish, not forgetting that sometimes lightness in a wine can be successful with heavy food

✘ Expect light wines to provide a good match to strong flavours

Dryness and Sweetness

✔ Think about ripeness of fruit - wines with ripe 'sweetness' that are actually dry. Consider wines with some sweetness with vegetables, e.g. carrots (which have a sweetness of their own). Select a sweet wine as sweet as a pudding

✘ Serve dry wines with sweets

Tannin

✔ Bear in mind the softening effect that food has on wines with tannin

✘ Pair red wines (high in tannin) with egg-based dishes, celery or spinach and spicy food

Intensity of Flavour

✔ Match richly flavoured dishes with concentrated wines

✘ Serve intense wines with subtle flavours

Oak

✔ Try oaked wines with smoked fish or meat

✘ In general, serve oaked wines with spicy dishes

Buttery Flavours

✔ Bridge the gap between richness in food and in wines

✘ Serve buttery, rich wines, with simply prepared and flavoured dishes

Cooking with Wine

Wine can add colour, richness, acidity and body to sauces, stews, soups, and casseroles. It is also an ingredient in many marinades. To be successful, a wine should not be completely devoid of fruit or, even worse, faulty. Neither does it have to be the best bottle in the cellar. Research shows however, that the better the wine, the better the final result.

If you are looking for a successful match between the wine in your glass and the wine in a dish, it makes sense to use a wine with similar characteristics. A good cook will consider the individual facets of a wine before incorporating it into a dish. Alcohol will be boiled off when added to a hot pan but care should be taken when making iced desserts as, if too much wine is added, alcohol will lower the freezing point and the dessert may not set.

Sweet Wines

When using sweet wines, or any wine with an element of sweetness, the flavour will intensify as the sauce cooks and reduces. Taste, to make sure that the wine you are about to drink has the same degree of sweetness as the sauce. Remember too, that fruit and vegetables, such as tomatoes, carrots, onions and garlic, will reveal sweetness when cooked. Tomatoes also contain acidity, so look for complementary characteristics in a wine.

If cooking with a white wine which has fairly crisp acidity, remember that the acidity also intensifies as it cooks. If your sauce becomes too acidic, adjust by adding cream or butter.

Dishes

Some dishes rely very much on wine as an ingredient, for example boeuf bourgignon and coq au vin. The wine adds a richness and intensity of flavour to the dish. However, highly flavoured or aromatic and oaked wines are often best avoided. Aromatics are lost very quickly once the wine begins to boil, while oak does not evaporate, but the oak flavour concentrates as it reduces, rendering a sauce possibly too powerful for the food.

If you keep leftover wine, or have a separate supply for cooking purposes, use a wine preserver to keep it in good condition. Keeping bottles in the refrigerator will also help to retain an element of freshness.

COOKING WITH WINE

Vintages

Vintages should only be used as a general guide. They only really apply to the very best wines where personality can vary. Some wine-producing countries and regions show very little change in consistency from one year to the next. Regions in northerly areas, deemed as cool climate, or those which are subject to marginal climates, show much more variation over a given period.

Vintage Ratings

1–3 Poor vintages. Only the top properties are likely to have made reasonable wines

4–7 Average to above average. Some red wines may be more accessible in youth

8–10 Great to outstanding

FRANCE
Alsace

Vintage	1990	1991	1992	1993	1994	1995	1996	1997	1998	1999	2000	2001
	9	2	5	6	7	5	7	7	7	6	9	8

Bordeaux

Bordeaux wines are mostly blended with the grape varieties which ripen at different times. The Merlot-dominated Right Bank should be viewed separately to the Cabernet-dominated Left Bank.

Vintage	1990	1991	1992	1993	1994	1995	1996	1997	1998	1999	2000	2001
Red Wines (Médoc/ Left Bank)	10	3	1	4	6	8	9	5	6	7	10	7
Red Wines (St Emilion & Pomerol/ Right Bank)	10	1	3	4	6	8	7	5	10	7	10	7
Dry Whites	8	4	5	4	8	7	8	6	8	8	8	9
Sweet Whites	10	3	1	1	3	5	9	9	8	8	4	10

Earlier successful sweet white vintages.

Vintage	1989	1988	1986	1985	1983
	8	9	9	8	9

Burgundy

Vintage	1990	1991	1992	1993	1994	1995	1996	1997	1998	1999	2000	2001
White	6	7	5	4	5	8	8	7	5	8	7	8
Red	9	8	5	7	5	7	7	7	6	9	6	4
Chablis	-	-	-	-	-	8	9	7	6	8	9	3
Beaujolais	-	-	-	-	-	7	4	5	4	9	9	4

FRANCE
The Loire Valley

Vintage	1995	1996	1997	1998	1999	2000	2001
Dry white	8	9	5	6	7	8	6
Red	8	9	7	5	7	7	5
Sweet wine	8	9	8	5	5	6	7

Earlier successful sweet wine vintages	
1990	9
1989	9
1988	8
1986	8
1985	8

The Rhône Valley

Vintage	1990	1991	1992	1993	1994	1995	1996	1997	1998	1999	2000	2001
North	10	8	1	2	6	7	6	8	9	10	8	8
South	10	4	3	4	6	7	5	5	10	8	9	8

Champagne

Only the best vintages are listed and those which are likely to be still available or maturing in cellar.

Vintage	1985	1988	1989	1990	1995	1996
	9	9	8	9	8	9

GERMANY

The late 1980s and the 1990s was an extremely favourable period for German wines. Wines from the Riesling grape have the capacity to age very well.

Vintage	1989	1990	1991	1992	1993	1994	1995	1996	1997	1998	1999	2000	2001
Mosel	9	9	6	7	8	8	9	7	9	8	9	7	10
Rhine	8	9	6	7	7	6	8	8	9	8	9	7	9

ITALY

Only the best recent vintages are listed.

Vintage	1989	1990	1995	1996	1997	1998	1999	2000	2001
Piedmont Reds	9	9	6	8	8	9	9	8	8
Tuscan Reds	-	9	6	6	9	7	9	8	8

SPAIN

Vintage	1994	1995	1996	1997	1998	1999	2000
Rioja	9	8	8	6	7	7	7

USA

Vintage	1996	1997	1998	1999	2000
White	9	8	6	8	7
Red	8	9	7	8	7

AUSTRALIA

Vintage	1996	1997	1998	1999	2000	2001
White	5	9	8	7	8	8
Red	9	7	8	9	7	8

NEW ZEALAND

Vintage	1998	1999	2000	2001
White	7	8	8	8
Red	9	7	7	7

SOUTH AFRICA

Vintage	1998	1999	2000	2001
White	7	8	8	7
Red	8	7	6	9

Glossary & Reference

Acidity The essential natural component which gives wine freshness and zing and prevents it cloying.

Aftertaste The taste that lingers after the wine has been tasted.

Aroma The particular smell of a grape variety.

Artificial Used to describe wines, part of whose taste appears to have been created chemically. Also contrived, confected.

Astringent A characteristic mostly found in young, red wine. Creates a tactile sensation on the palate.

Attack An immediate effect which makes you sit up and take notice.

Austere A wine which seems difficult to approach, whose fruit isn't immediately apparent.

Balance A balanced wine has its fruitiness, acidity, alcohol and tannin (for reds) in pleasant harmony. An unbalanced wine has too much of one or more of these. Balance may develop with age.

Barrel/Bottle age The length of time a wine has spent in barrel/bottle.

Blanc de blancs White wine, particularly Champagne, made only from white grapes.

Blending Mixing together different wines.

Body A full-bodied wine fills the mouth with flavour. Can also be described as being full, or having weight.

Botrytis The 'noble rot' of great sweet white wines. A welcome mould which can creep over ripe grapes at the end of the summer, enabling winemakers to produce the finest sweet white wines in the world, most notably Sauternes and Trockenbeerenauslese.

Bouquet The overall smell of a wine, often made up of several separate aromas.

Buttery The rich smell – literally the smell of fresh butter – often found in good Chardonnay wines and sometimes associated with wine which has been left on its lees.

Cabernet Sauvignon The great Bordeaux Left Bank grape.

Chaptalisation The process of adding sugar to must to increase the alcoholic degree of the finished wine.

Chardonnay The great white Burgundy and Champagne grape.

Chenin Blanc The leading white grape of the Loire.

Claret English term for red wine from Bordeaux.

Clean A wine which smells and tastes of fruit.

Clos A wall-enclosed vineyard.

Cloying The characteristic of poor sweet wines. A sickly flavour.

Coarse Probably badly made, rough-tasting wine.

Complex Some wines have interesting and complex mixtures of smells and flavours. Multidimensional.

Corked The unpleasant, musty smell and flavour caused by an affected cork.

Crisp Fresh wine, with good acidity.

Cuve close Sparkling wine created by re-fermenting the wine in closed tanks rather than in bottles.

Demi sec Medium to sweet.

Domaine Estate.

Dumb As in 'Dumb Nose' – meaning no apparent smell.

Finish Wine can taste very different when you first put it in to your mouth from the way it does just before you spit it out or swallow it. The finish is the aftertaste.

Flabby Lacking balancing acidity.

Flor Yeast that grows on the surface of some wines, protecting the wine from the air.

Fortified wine Wine which has grape spirit added before fermentation is complete.

Gamay The only grape for red Beaujolais.

Gamey A meaty smell, reminiscent of hung game.

Gewürztraminer Aromatic, spicy white grape variety.

Grenache Peppery flavoured Rhône grape variety.

Hot Highly alcoholic wine can be 'hot', either because of high natural sugar in the harvested grapes (e.g. from a hot climate), or poor winemaking.

Late harvest Late-harvested grapes contain more sugar and concentrated flavours.

Lie (or lees) The solid matter (yeast etc.) which drops to the bottom of casks or vats of newly-made wine.

Length The length of time bouquet and flavour linger after swallowing.

Macération Carbonique (or whole berry fermentation) The method of winemaking used for Beaujolais and some other young-drinking wines by which the grapes begin to ferment, uncrushed and oxygen-free, beneath a layer of carbon dioxide.

Merlot The soft Bordeaux grape (Right Bank).

Methode Champenoise The method of sparkling wine production used in Champagne.

Mousse The sparkle in fizzy wine.

Müller-Thurgau Early ripening, high-yielding white grape variety.

Muscat Perfumed grape variety. Generally for sweet wines.

Must Unfermented grape juice.

Négociant Merchant who buys in wine from growers and bottles it for sale.

Nose Smell or aroma.

Oaky The flavour imparted by oak casks.

Oxidised Wine the air has 'got at' and destroyed.

Palate The taste, and what you taste with.

Petrol A not unpleasant overtone often found in maturing Riesling.

Phylloxera Bug which attacks vine roots.

Pinot Noir The great grape of red Burgundy and Champagne.

Racy Crisp, lively wine.

Riesling Noblest of the German grapes.

Sauvignon Blanc The great grape of the upper Loire and New Zealand. Called Fumé Blanc in America.

Sec Dry.

Sémillon The luscious grape of great Sauternes.

Soft Smooth, mellow, easy-to-drink, not hard.

Spritz Slight sparkle, or faint fizz, also called Pétillant.

Stalky (or Stemmy) The flavour of the stem rather than the juice.

Steely Firm, characterful wine with good acidity.

Structure Wine with good structure is like a well-designed building: all parts fit together harmoniously. Wine with poor structure is probably falling apart.

Sulphur dioxide Bacteria-killing chemical used in winemaking. Over-sulphured wines can smell of bad eggs and may irritate the back of the throat when sniffed.

Sur lie 'On the lees' Wine bottled straight from the fermentation vat or cask to impart extra taste.

Shiraz (Syrah) Deep-coloured, smoky-flavoured Rhône grape.

Tannin The substance in red wine which comes from the grape skins, stems, and pips and gives the mouth-drying sensation. Necessary for red wine to age.

Tart Generally over-acid.

Terroir The term used to describe the growing conditions of the grape, such as the soil, drainage, microclimate, and exposure to the sun.

Tired (or tiring) Wine which has seen better days.

Tröcken Dry.

Varietal Used to describe wines made from specific grape varieties, sold under the name of those grapes e.g. Australian 'Chardonnay'.

Vielles vignes Wines from mature vines.

Vin de pays The lowest category of French wine – 'country wine'.

Vinification Turning grapes into wine.

Vintage A single year's grape harvest; the wine of a single year.

Yeast Organism that causes grape juice to ferment.

Zinfandel Quirky American grape variety.

GLOSSARY AND REFERENCE

Varieties & Characteristics of White Grapes

SAUVIGNON
(SAUVIGNON BLANC –FUMÉ BLANC)

Wine styles: dry, high acidity, aromatic, herby, grassy, and sometimes smoky scented wine. Blends well with Sémillon
Regions: Loire, Bordeaux, New Zealand, California, Australia, Chile and South Africa

SÉMILLON

Wine styles: lowish acidity, soft, good sugars, subject to noble rot
Regions: Bordeaux (dry and sweet), Australia (Hunter Valley)

CHARDONNAY

Wine styles: dry – produces a range of flavours including pineapple, lemon, biscuit, butter and vanilla (when oak aged). Can be extremely complex. Technically dry, classic grape for Champagne
Regions: Burgundy, South of France, Champagne, Australia, California, New Zealand, Chile, South Africa and Bulgaria

RIESLING

Wine styles: brilliant, sweet–acid balance, flowery in youth, with subtle, oily scents when mature, often low in alcohol. Subject to noble rot. Dry, medium, and sweet
Regions: Germany, Alsace, Austria, Australia, California, New Zealand and South Africa

CHENIN BLANC

Wine styles: high acidity, dry – taking on honeyed character when mature. Subject to noble rot. Can be sparkling
Regions: Loire (Vouvray/Layon) etc., South Africa, New Zealand, Australia and California

PINOT BLANC

*Wine styles: dry, soft, full, honeyed,
or crisp, still or fizzy*
Regions: north Italy, Alsace and
southern Germany

PINOT GRIS

*Wine styles: fat, alcoholic, spicy, honeyed,
dry to sweet*
Regions: Alsace, northeast Italy, eastern
Europe, New Zealand and Washington State

MUSCADET

*Wine styles: when sur lie it is dry, tangy,
bready, with high acidity*
Regions: France – the Loire

VIOGNIER

*Wine styles: dry, fruity, aromatic, apricot
flavoured, subtle, complex, to drink young.
Some sweet late harvest*
Regions: northern Rhone, south of France
and California

GEWÜRZTRAMINER

*Wine styles: full-bodied, spicy and
aromatic, dry to very sweet*
Regions: Alsace, northeast Italy, USA,
Austria, Germany and New Zealand

MUSCAT

*Wine styles: floral, grapey, dry to sweet,
can be fortified*
Regions: Alsace, south of France,
northeast Italy, Australia and elsewhere

MARSANNE

Wine styles: dry, rich and oily, peachy, nutty
Regions: Rhône, south of
France and Australia

VERDELHO

*Wine styles: aromatic, tropical, and
citrus fruits*
Regions: Madeira and Australia

GLOSSARY AND
REFERENCE

Varieties & Characteristics of Red Grapes

PINOT NOIR

Wine styles: can produce brilliant scents, texture, flavour and body. Blends sweet fruit with savoury complexity. Can be sparkling
Regions: Burgundy, Champagne, Alsace, Sancerre, Germany, northern Italy, Switzerland, California, Oregon, Australia and New Zealand

GAMAY

Wine styles: fragrant, fruity, youthful, low tannin
Regions: Beaujolais, Loire, Switzerland

CABERNET SAUVIGNON

Wine styles: spicy, herby, tannic with characteristic blackcurrant aroma. Blends well with Merlot or Shiraz
Regions: Bordeaux (Medoc), California, Australia, South America, South Africa and Washington State

BARBERA

Wine styles: medium to full-bodied, sweet/sour-flavoured fruit with highish acidity
Regions: Italy, Argentina, Australia and California

MERLOT

Wine styles: fragrant, fruity and soft. Generally low tannin
Regions: Bordeaux (Pomerol and St Emilion), California, northern Italy, South America and South Africa

SHIRAZ/SYRAH

Wine styles: rich flavoured, smoky, tarry and spicy. Tannic when young
Regions: Rhône Valley (northern), southern France, Australia, California, South America and South Africa

MOURVÈDRE (MONASTRELL, MATARO)

Wine styles: rich, damson-like fruits, powerful
Regions: southern Rhône, south of France, Spain, Australia and California

CABERNET FRANC

Wine styles: 'grassy', raspberry fruit, with highish acidity
Regions: the Loire, Bordeaux, northern Italy and Australia

GRENACHE

Wine styles: spicy, peppery, strawberry-scented, red and rosé
Regions: southern Rhône, south of France, Spain and Australia

TEMPRANILLO

Wine styles: wild strawberry, combining with herby, savoury, tobacco-like characteristics
Regions: Rioja, Ribera del Duero (Spain) and Argentina

SANGIOVESE

Wine styles: top vines produce concentrated reds with pronounced tannin and acidity. When mature, cedary, plummy fruit flavours are apparent
Regions: Tuscany, Romagna, and Marche (Italy) and Argentina

NEBBIOLO

Wine styles: traditionally tannic that requires ageing, or a lighter, fruity, modern style with less tannin.
At best, savoury and complex
Regions: Piedmonte-Barolo and Barbaresco (Italy) and Australia (Victoria)

ZINFANDEL

Wine styles: 'White Zin' to red. Best from old vines, oak aged, rich with blackberry fruit flavours, peppery and tangy acidity
Regions: California

PINOTAGE

Wine styles: often sweet thick, can have overstated esters on the nose. Best are concentrated and earthy
Regions: South Africa and New Zealand

CARMENÈRE

Wine styles: deep colour, red pepper aromas, lush, blackberry, blueberry, chocolate flavours
Regions: Chile and Bordeaux

GLOSSARY AND REFERENCE

Conclusion

Most of what we eat and drink is in danger of becoming a mass-produced product, lacking any sense of place or individuality.

Thank goodness therefore, for wines that change with each vintage and winemakers who truly believe in expressing terroir, as well as their own personality, in their wines. Unfortunately though, these individuals are in the minority and so are some of the world's more unusual, yet fascinating grape varieties.

What a shame it would be if growers in parts of Spain, for example, increasingly felt under pressure to grow non-Spanish varieties, in preference to Tempranillo. If the Portuguese shifted the emphasis towards international grapes and used a standard recipe in order to satisfy the marketeers and accountants, would

it matter? Do we care? Appreciating wine comes in many forms, but surely one of the great pleasures is to find the unusual, the unexpected and a flavour sensation that lives in the memory.

Buying a bottle from a conscientious grower, so proud of their product, can help safeguard their future and the raw material that they have at their disposal. As more and more multinational companies flex their financial muscle in the world of wine, sadly we can expect to see more brands dominating shelf space and wine lists. On a positive note, wine tourism appears to be increasingly popular, bringing together the liquid in the glass and the culture, often interacting in some of the world's most stunning visual locations.

Kind thanks to
Lay & Wheeler International Wine Merchants
www.laywheeler.com
for assisting in some of the photography in this book